The Train Blog

Odd and Weird People Watching

By Ted Smith

Published by EMR Smith

ISBN: 9798639051296

Cover design by: Valentina Rinaldi
Edited by: Elizabeth Baker

Dedications
I'd like to thank all my friends who have encouraged me to publish this for the past five years. It is dedicated to the medical and care workers who are losing their lives to Covid19. All profits will go charities supporting them.

To Valentina Rinaldi for illustrating the front cover (based on the events of 3 August 2016 – see later), whilst in lockdown in Northern Italy.

To Elizabeth Baker, a future journalist or writer in the making, for proof reading my awful text and teaching me English.

To Tracy Smith for putting up with my late nights and odd behaviour, especially as this got closer to publication, and to Tom and James Smith, for keeping me in good humour from the front line in New Zealand.

Introduction

I should probably have taken a degree in behavioural studies at college, but instead I've decided that it's much more fun as an amateur hobby instead.

I travel in and out of London quite a bit. I'll read the odd newspaper, play a game on my phone, but most of all I love to watch what other people get up to, and then write short blogs about it.

This is a collection of those blogs over the years. Brought together now, to try and raise some funds for the NHS Charities Together Appeal, at a time when our doctors, nurses and healthcare workers are struggling with the ravages of a deadly virus (not "just" the 'flu'), on top of years of under-funding from a Government that is overly-fond of supporting the private sector.

This is my first book, and it has been pulled-together, at speed, to start making some money for the charities.

A properly edited and typeset book on Human Resources will follow later in the year, as well as a couple of children's short stories, proving that some good can come from adversity and covid-19 lockdown.

I have used Kindle and Amazon self-publishing, simply to get it to market quickly, not because I have any fond thoughts about companies that operate on a global scale. Traditional agents, editors, publishers and printers need months in which to convert text to books (unless you're a footballer that has just coughed, of course).

The Train Blog

16 April 2013

"We have a traveling chef on board the train today, which means we can serve porridge and bacon baguettes". In other words, he has been trained how to add hot water to a plastic pot and stir, as well as use the microwave! Yummy.

27 August 2013

Another rubbish experience with First Capital Connect. Over-running engineering work, means delays and packed trains all day. As ever no explanations and the staff are clueless, due to poor management and next to no communications from Head Office.

28 October 2013

First Crapita Disconnect (as I now like to call them) - the only service to cancel all its trains before the storm started and to fail to give any real updates; just bland nonsense about advice not to travel, no evidence as usual, and so the worst communications award goes to...

31 January 2014

Two questions for fellow sufferers on the line from Welwyn Garden City to Kings Cross: 1. Have you ever sat on a seat and found that it was both clean, and didn't fall apart? And 2. Do you all lose the Internet when sat at Hatfield station? (What is it about Hatfield?)

19 September 2014

Another day, and another broken down train. Three full refund claims in three weeks. Govia may have taken over the franchise from FCC but there is absolutely no benefit as a passenger.

16 July 2015
Today breaks all records. I am sat with five women in a six-seater section of the train. All of them, all, are using their phones as mirrors as they apply their make-up. All five. Arrrrrghhhh! Suggestions please as to the most-manly thing I should do in response?

25 July 2015
A somewhat horrendous journey from Heidelberg to Frankfurt Flughaven today. Natasha Gordon and I had visited the European Molecular Biology Laboratories up in the hills overlooking the beautiful old city of Heidelberg, and I had the great idea that we would save a lot of money (and the environment) by taking a couple of trains to the airport, rather than a taxi.

The first train was running late. It travelled at ridiculously slow speeds and kept stopping, with unintelligible announcements. It was, of course, a heatwave, and there was no aircon, but also no windows or vents. After a while it was announced that we would be stopping at a town we had never heard of. I google mapped it and announced that the only way out of the dilemma was to get off the train, and that if we ran (with all our bags) over the bridge to the other side we could catch a faster connecting train and still, hopefully, get to the airport in time. We got off, ran up and over the bridge, but the train either never showed up, or had already gone, and by now our slow train was long gone.

Eventually another slow train came along and we boarded that, but without any real idea where it was going. It again was stopping everywhere. So, we started looking out of the window for a train station with a taxi rank. We ran to the taxi, bartered for an only mildly ridiculous fare and made the terminal with minutes to spare, only to discover that the plane home was delayed as well!

31 August 2015
As I sit on the train "enjoying" my commute into London, I'm
reflecting on a short holiday in Sicily, and would like to offer
these tips to anyone considering driving there:
* Top tip: he who hesitates is hit
* Side roads: are motorways in disguise
* Motorways: try to stay no more than two, and no less than
three inches from the car in front
* One-way streets: it's a loose guideline
* Roundabouts: everyone has priority
* Speed limits: old people drive at half the limit, young twice,
there is no middle age
* Motorcycles: there are no rules or guidelines, they are
invincible and own every road and footway
* Pedestrians: Zebra crossings are art works, they serve no
functional purpose
* Pedestrian only zone: another name for a motorway
* Motorway breakfast: brioche filled with Pistachio ice cream
* Pavements/Sidewalks: are additional car parking spaces when
the road is already double parked
* Parking bays: are sometimes empty between 03.00 and 03.01

Perhaps more scarily, I have to thank Fiat from providing auto-
locking on the doors of the 500 model that we rented. It
prevented us from being robbed or car-jacked. What
happened? As we approached a motorway slip-road, a scooter
pulled out of a side road in front of us, and stopped quickly. I
instinctively jammed on the brakes to avoid hitting it.
Meanwhile another scooter came-up to the passenger door and
tried to open it. The door was locked, so the driver threw a
finger at us and disappeared with his mate up another road. I
was unable to identify either of them, with full face helmet and
no registration plates, so that was it. How different it could
have been though....

18 September 2015

The 18.22 out of Kings Cross comprises just 4 coaches, due to "mechanical issues", and the previous train to Peterborough was cancelled. It's rather full, as in sardines have a better life even though they are dead. But the good news? The heating is full-on and can't be turned down on the third hottest day of the year!

30 September 2015

Every so often I "treat myself" to the slow train. It starts from my station and stops everywhere along the line. I am guaranteed a seat (which is not the case on the fast train which starts further up the line), but I lose 15 to 20 minutes.

I get the joy of watching people as they slowly fill-up the carriage. Always looking to seat themselves as far apart as the remaining space will allow. They're either trying not to look at each other, hiding behind the Metro newspaper, or playing on their phones.

These rules are, of course, broken by overseas visitors and the socially unadjusted. So just now a young guy wearing a man-dress-trouser-thingy (Beckham from ten years ago), playing music through his fake Beats headphones, so loudly that everyone ended-up staring daggers at him, was cheered when he got off the train after just a few stops.

And by way of celebration a very rare thing happened, for a full minute people were chatting to each other :-). It's ok though, all is now back to normal, but it has made my day .... Added to the news that a man called Thwaites is recounting how he lived as a goat in the Alps in a clip I'm reading - funded by the Wellcome Trust!

6 October 2015

I've been fighting umbrellas for years in London streets, and I've been fighting selfie sticks for most of the summer months.

Today in the rain I fought a man wielding a selfie stick with an umbrella. I won. Ha!

22 October 2015

Today's journey into work is worthy of mention. Not because I got a seat (yesterday Great Northern could only find three working carriages and today there are eight), but because the woman who sat opposite me not only managed to apply three full layers of make-up, as well as lipstick and eye-lash stuff, but she also managed to chat constantly to her friend for the whole 20 minutes. I kid you not.

The friend's contribution was to say ugh, mm, yep. Not even "oh I know". 20 minutes without hesitation, repetition .... but sadly, also without any interest to those of us forced to listen. Tomorrow I must remember to have my head phones with me. 20 minutes! 20. Venus. Mars.

27 October 2015

Thoughts on the commute in Malawi .... For those of you who have commented on my first world problems commuting in the UK by train, moving between sites here has been interesting for different reasons.

Today we had to slow up (and sometimes stop) for: a chicken and her chicks crossing the road, lots of random goats, a huge cow, a man riding a bike with half a tree sticking out at the back, women balancing 80 litre water carriers on their heads, children playing on their way to/from school, a lorry driving in the middle of a mountain road at 2mph, a man running-out in front of us whilst waving a lot, several police road blocks, an entirely pointless foot and mouth blockade where we had to get out of the car to stand on a disinfected mat and then get back in via the contaminated soil, mango sellers, a mum with a baby front and back, a road to the hospital so bumpy that I needed the hospital and ..... Well the list goes on. It's certainly interesting here in Africa's poorest country.

2 November 2015
You know you're back in the UK when you wake to dank, dark fog and dripping trees, a tad different to Malawi (where it was me that was dripping with sweat, being so unaccustomed to the heat).

And so, to the train journey. Quite full today, with some interesting characters. No-one doing their makeup, but three Dom Jolly phone calls. Why do people think they need to shout extra loud into a phone when on the train? But the classic is a woman who had a big sneeze - all over the people opposite. She then shouts "BLESS ME!" - I don't think I've ever heard that before? No apology for the sneeze. She then says "that's better" and puts the Dr Dre cans back on - which had fallen off. Everyone else is now giving her the evil eye!!!

4 November 2015
Spoiler: this is a disappointing train journey post.

I've just had a normal train journey, i.e. delayed ("severe delay due to lost crew member"). I do hope they find him/her - or maybe they have and that's why we now have a train? No-one is doing their make-up. No noisy headphones. Several hushed normal conversations. No slavering dogs. No puking kids. No loud phone calls. No partridges in a pear tree (even though John Lewis had one in September for goodness sake).

Amazingly the temperature is neither too hot nor too cold, and the rain isn't getting in through the window. People are only standing near the doors. No-one looks like a model; they are all dressed appropriately for a day in the office. Even the driver that they found is speaking clearly, and is very informative. The standard, slightly confused and concerned foreign traveller has been kept under control by a lovely lady who keeps telling him what the next station is, and that the stop he wants is at the end of the line (it's called London).

Yesterday I was asked if I had a vivid imagination. I said yes, but that I simply didn't have to deploy it when writing about my experiences ..... It normally writes itself. Hopefully my next trip will feature something worthy of a post.

19 November 2015

As I sit contemplating whether I should try to finish my somewhat substandard and overcooked chicken dinner at the motorway service station, I can at least rest easy that I am not in a hospital bed being subjected to their revamped "daily dietary offering". My mum is a vegetarian, so I was somewhat surprised to be asked to help feed her meal to her tonight... I'll go through the hospital menu.

To start an appetizer. A small tub of "Pure Apple Juice with Apple", featuring a lid that no-one has yet mastered, let alone the people in the geriatric ward who don't have strong fingers. Heat welded at 2000 degrees C to pasteurize any life out of the apple, the lid is so well sealed on that the act of opening it sprays most of the contents over the tray.

The main course. Beef lasagne. I explain that my mum is vegetarian, to which the catering lady says, and I quote, "can you scrape-out the meat so that she has the vegetarian bit please?". Honestly! The side dish is very, very mashed potato - to achieve this please take a potato and boil it overnight, then pulverize it, then leave in a fridge for four days, then mash it again and then leave to reach room temperature and then reheat in a microwave and finally serve it with a piece of greenery taken from the nearest pot plant. It is claggy and well disgusting, and didn't pass the mum test. My Labrador eats anything, I'm tempted to take some home to see if Tess will also reject it!

And for pudding - the most edible thing on offer? Raspberry and Vanilla moose in a plastic pot with an easily removable lid! I thought this would be the winner with mum, but no, apparently it "tastes yuk". So, I tried it and you know what, that is a polite description of what I imagine eating bleached excrement with added food flavourings would taste like.

All I can say is that it is a good job that I had a Nak'd berry bar in my pocket. That became Miranda's meal for the night. Washed down with finest *eau de tap*. All this makes the food served on trains these days seem simply delightful.

27 November 2015
Faith restored in train conversations. Four students chatting in the seats next to me. They discussed Trump. They couldn't believe that Americans were still supporting him, given how he has made direct verbal assaults on so many minority groups and was so clearly the wrong person to run the country.

Then a longer debate about Corbyn. Delight that he was holding firm, but concern that he was losing so much support. The exact opposite of Trump. Slagged off the Mao red book trick as lame, couldn't believe that Osbourne had 'u'- turned on everything and then they moved on to climate change. Cool!

No-one has done their make-up. No-one has sneezed all over me. One guy with a cough, but all contained. Train is only 8 minutes late because we are following a slower train, but the heating level is appropriate, even if the toilets are not working. And the man with the bike has stood holding it all journey, so it hasn't randomly traversed the carriage.

1 December 2015
Trains. I've had a large number of requests (well 3 actually) to put finger to screen and keep up my train blog work. Today's starts with the walk to the station. Two foxes ahead standing facing and snarling at each other, oblivious of my approach. I

got within ten yards before one ran away and the other followed.

As I got closer, I was trying to work out what sex they were. I couldn't see any low hanging tackle - but maybe it's hidden? Can anyone help - what are the differentiating characteristics between a fox and a vixen?

So, before I get to the train itself, the train is delayed. Depressingly there is no reason given. I love hearing the latest invention - especially when the station announcer gives a different reason to the automated sign board, which in turn is different to the train driver's garbled reasoning. Usually it is as follows: boards say delayed due to lack of staff, station announcer says it's due to leaves on the track and driver says it's because he was following a slow train. That is the winning 3-way combo if you're into betting, Roy Heyward.

A delayed train gives me an excuse to get a tea or coffee whilst I wait. Since the tea is almost the same price (and yet involves chucking a bag in and adding hot water), I prefer to make them earn my money by asking for a coffee. Black Americano is the order. I am the only person there. The older lady who runs the café has popped-out and the young girl looks perplexed. But instead of asking for advice she decides to get on with it, and produces a near perfect Cappuccino. She asks if I want chocolate sprinkles? I explain that I want a simple Black Americano, which is a shot of coffee topped up by hot water. "Oh yeah, but I have made this".

My train saved the day by managing to un-delay itself, no doubt due to "traveling downhill from the north to south" or "using the fast lane to get round the slow train" or "a tail wind that also removed the leaves". I decided not to fight and enjoy the coffee with chocolate sprinkles. "If you use your card, then I have to surcharge you" ... "But you can let me off as you have given me the wrong coffee" .... "I'll have to ask my manager" ....

"It's ok I will leave it with you, I want to get on the train that's just arriving".... "Oh ok, have a nice day".

And so, to the train. It's half empty. I get a seat. It's firm and fixed and doesn't fall off. It's clean with no gum on it. The person opposite is asleep and not snoring. All is good. Until we get to Hatfield, which sadly is the next stop.

As I now type, I am surrounded by six rah-rah girls who apparently share a house in Hatfield, but attend the Royal Veterinary College. They are so "ok yah", and so loud and so full of themselves, that I now really regret being coffee-less. "I'm so looking forward to seeing Jessica today" one starts. It's only later I realize she is talking about an injured horse. I swear I thought she was talking about massaging a best friend when she first mentioned it!!!!!! Just in case anyone's interested, it's Jonty's birthday tomorrow and they are going to surprise her by covering her car with straw. It sounds so spiffing!

3rd December 2015
Lots of traveling today. At least ten parts to the journey - so I will make a start. Up early and on a much earlier train into London - meaning that there is absolutely no chance of meeting the trainee vets and asking what Colin thought about dog foxes and vixens. Maybe tomorrow. This train is packed, but quiet. When it's this early a lot of people just want to sleep. I'm one of the few using a mobile. Even the newspapers are resting on laps.

The first leg though has been dominated by alarms going off. According to the older lady in the coffee shop (who did know what a black Americano was) the alarm is in the shopping centre and has been going off since she started. "No" says the guy in the queue behind me - it's the car park. But no war kicks off, she just says "oh" and doesn't ask me if I want chocolate sprinkles.

The train arrived on time at Kings Cross. The weather was fine. I walked to Euston station. Roads already log jammed and exhaust pollution mounting. Stopped to buy a Big Issue, but the poor woman sneezed all over her stock, so I left her the money but didn't take the magazine. Haven't been inside Euston for a while, but discovered that the food court has finally been closed. It must have been the point at which someone realized there were more rats than passengers in there. Upstairs to a temporary Leon's for porridge.

As I walk to the far end of platform 7 to catch my train to Coventry (being sent there in my school days used to cause a laugh), I have to pass a Virgin train that's going to Holyhead. It is closed-up, dark, no driver at either end and yet it has been left running. Huge amounts of diesel being wasted. I am going to read the Virgin trains website to find out what they are claiming re environmental responsibility.

An unremarkable journey on Virgin trains. Arrived in Coventry on time. No blog inspiration here at all so far! Virgin trains are so uninspiring. As are the taxis to Warwick University and back. Another three journeys and everyone was normal and boring. Next to Swindon. I used to do this trip all the time. And it isn't letting me down. 2.15pm and its full and we have a screaming baby, and a child who is already asking "are we there yet", after five minutes!

Having made it to Swindon, I have now transferred to The Cheltenham Flyer. This is obviously an ironic reference to the days of steam when 30mph was considered fast. It's a lovely little two carriage push me pull you. That's me being generous. Soooooo sloooooow. The train keeps blowing its horn. There's probably an apprentice up-front, walking ahead with a waved red flag. Just gone past Stonehouse - I could swear it said "replacement horse and cart service this way".

And so, I'm on the way home after a quick visit to see a poorly mum; I'm on the only train each day that seems to go direct from Cheltenham to London, lucky me. But no luck for the lady in the wheelchair who has just discovered that only two carriages of this train can actually reach the platform at Stonehouse! She was told at Cheltenham to get into E, but she needed to be in A or B. Jeez this is difficult.

12th leg of the journey today and first ticket check.

1 January 2016

Given that there is little to blog about on trains that are clean and punctual in Japan, I think I should mention Japanese TV instead. It's early morning here and I have flicked through 26 channels and analysed them for you.

There are 6 local/national news shows. Everything else is a game show except for pay movies. To be honest I can't differentiate between game shows for kids and game shows for adults. They all have a similar formula and feel to them.......

An event occurs - it could be a clip of one animal eating another, a semi human throwing themselves into a vat of custard, an extreme balancing act on a tall building whilst wearing a kimono, or just the person who could last longest whilst being hit with a bat.

The clip is shown, and then a group in the studio analyse the clip for about five minutes. They use slow motion replays and get very excited when someone's expression changes (e.g. when a toad jumps on the cat being held by a young child). Then an advert and the compere introduces the next, completely unrelated, bizarre clip. Repeat *ad nauseam*.

I have to say I was expecting some manga type cartoon shows. But on reflection they are probably not suitable for the young audience at this time of day......

11 January 2016
David Bowie has died.

12 January 2016
Yesterday I didn't manage to write very much. I just sat and listened to Blackstar by Bowie. I've been to see him 5 times, including seeing him as a Spider from Mars, as Aladdin Sane, as the Thin White Duke and met him briefly on the Reality Tour. I'm no super fan, but I am going to miss his creativity.

29 January 2016
Three strange and inexplainable things have happened so far today and it's still only 07.30. Firstly, I plugged in a device with mini USB power and the plug went straight in, I didn't have to turn it around several times. Second, my train arrived at the platform on time. Third, I got a seat. *Feeling blessed*.

2 February 2016
One of those days when the earlier train is so delayed that it becomes the fast train. But the phrase "standing room only" doesn't adequately describe the conditions that we had to travel under. I'm struggling to understand how the announcement from our train operator (that they will run shorter, but new trains) will help the situation.... But I guess if they run on time and have air con that will be a start. If only a Japanese or Swiss train operator would take on the franchise.

4 February 2016
This morning I had the pleasure of a chat with a Japanese student on the train, who has just started part of a short PhD placement at the university in Hatfield. He had a train timetable in his hand, and was struggling with matching the printed times with what was actually happening. I explained that in Japan train timetables were an exact science and that I had enjoyed my experiences on their tracks, but that in the UK they were

treated as a very rough guide to what might happen on a good day, but that good days were rare.

I explained that we have rails and overhead cables that expand in the heat and contract in the cold at rates that our engineers just cannot predict. I explained that signals might look pretty as they change colour, but that most times drivers have to go slowly whilst they phone their control room to check they are allowed to make progress. I explained that the trains are so old that they have preservation orders on them and are not allowed to be replaced. I explained that staffing levels are kept at a low level and cannot cope with flu seasons, holidays etc.

He didn't understand.

10 February 2016

For the past week or so my journey to the station has been far more interesting than the actual train journey. Not because of the early morning joggers (or in one case yesterday a limper), not because of the dog walkers allowing their "he's not normally like that" pedigree fluff ball to jump up at me, not because of the flickering street lights that have long since given up any hope of being cared for by the much reduced highways department, not because of the cracked pavements and random puddles, nor the speeding cars, nor the delivery vans driving into the shop front (well it was Specsavers) but......

Could someone please let me know where in the new Highway Code it encourages adult cyclists to attempt the land speed record on the pavement when a perfectly adequate road is right next to it? As a kid I was told off by the local beat Bobby for cycling on the pavement and I learned my lesson!

Three times in two weeks I have nearly been knocked over by the same cyclist who shoots past me, and having got parallel with me (i.e. too late) rings his pathetic little bell. This morning I was more on my guard and I left the house a bit earlier, and I clocked that he is mid-thirties, trainer beard, helmet, no lights turned on and, the good news, is on a Road Racing bike, which means his tires are thin!

I'm therefore looking for ideas from you all. My first thought is to fix a GoPro on my back and watch through my phone, and just as he gets close deploy a stinger of some sort (I'll need to see what B&Q have that would work). Or I could pad up and step to the side at the right moment or, maybe, suddenly change my rucksack (n.b. need to buy one) from one side to the other?

12 February 2016

As I sit on Platform 3, my train of thought today is focused on a health minister who has declared that he intends to impose a new contract on the doctors. Just imagine the transport chaos if the same was done to train drivers.

There are acknowledged problems with the current NHS contracts and they need to be resolved, but isn't it right that if we want a full (as opposed to an emergency) service at weekends that we increase the amount of money that we put in, and increase the number of people working in the health service, rather than say that Saturday is now a normal work day, and that if you want to go out to the theatre or see a band, or join friends for a meal that starts at 7.30 or 8pm, that you have to book holiday in advance, because that's now part of your normal workday?

Given that the changes to payments for out of hours working will now decrease at a rate faster than the increase in base pay, leading to a net decrease in pay, is it any wonder that so many I know are actively looking at opportunities to move abroad? Especially when their Health Secretary is known to want to privatise the NHS (Guardian 10/2/16), enjoys making disparaging and arrogant remarks and doesn't practice what he preaches (try booking into a surgery with him out of hours!)

Sad times.... at least the train is only running 5 minutes late today.

29 February 2016
On the train to York. An hour in and the tea trolley shows up. It's a bit like a cheese shop sketch by Monty Python. Server has a very strong Jordie accent.

"Any drinks or food?"
Yes please, a tea and an egg sandwich please.
"I should of said (sic), I have no hot water."
What soft drinks do you have?
"Do you mean alcohol?"
No, not really.
"Not much really left."
How about a Coke or a Fanta Orange?
"No."
Water?
"Yes, only cold, no hot."
Sparkling water please.
"We only have Abbey Well."
That's fine, thanks.
(Searches trolley) "Sorry, none left."
Ok - what do you have.?
"Irn-Bru, it's very popular."
No thanks.
"So, did you still want an egg sandwich?"
Yes please.
"I've got a breakfast roll with egg in it."
No, it's fine, thanks for trying, I'll wait till York.
"Oh yes, I do have a Yorkie Bar" ....
Maybe it was my fancy accent?

12 March 2016

As I sit on the train, I see an advert for Lloyds Bank. My experience with them does not match the advertising, or their clever marketing. They have been incredibly unhelpful and obstructive. Time to vent.

My mum died mid-December. She left my sister and I with a key and written authority to open her Lloyds safe deposit box, with a note saying that it contains the will and deeds to her bungalow, amongst other stuff.

We go to Lloyds in Montpelier Cheltenham - "Oh the boxes were moved to the main town branch". At the town branch "the boxes are in a salt mine run by G4S and will have to be ordered, has your mum died?" Yes, she's died, we need to see the will. "Well you can't, those instructions are revoked at the moment of her passing" and "only the executors of the will can open the box". We believe that we have been named executors, but the will has those details in it, therefore let's order in the box and have a look. "You can't, unless you can prove you're the executors".

Catch 22. So, we employ a solicitor and get an order to retrieve the box. Lloyds/G4S can't find the box, later turns out it was still in Montpelier! They send it to Welwyn. It is sent via Madagascar we think, because it takes 5 weeks to arrive. Our solicitor attends the opening and asks to take a copy "you can only take a copy if you have grant of probate!" Nonsense says our solicitor, I can only grant probate after reading and working through the will! "Sorry, it's the rules!" She insists they phone their head office, eventually they see sense, but now 30 minutes of solicitors paid time later and she gets a copy but isn't allowed to review anything else because she isn't a named executor!

Un-believe-able is the politest word that I can use. Needless to say, my sister is switching her bank account!

26 March 2016
Not being on a train for this long weekend gives me a chance to comment on other things. How about PetPlan Insurance? When Tess was a puppy, we paid £21 a month fully comprehensive. Best cover at a good price we were told. 15 years later the bill was a whopping £91 a month with an involuntary excess of £135. Now granted, insurance tax played a part, but the fact is that as a dog gets older the ability to switch insurance companies diminishes and so you get stuck. Maybe self-insurance is the answer, or a really cheap insurance that only covers third party claims and major surgery?

30 March 2016 Tonight, I can't discuss trains. Just cattle trucks. Another set of cancellations for various excuses. Animal rights are being infringed again by UnGreat Northern.

31 March 2016
As my train leaves the station on time (!!!!!!!), here's a typical phone call from a financial institution's specialist bereavement team:

"Dear Edward, may we call you by your first name?"
"Yes, it's Ted" (even though I don't know you, and you still haven't said who you are, but I've already guessed as the only person who called me that is now dead.)
"Firstly, we just wanted to say how dreadfully sorry we were to hear of your loss, the whole team here broke down and cried uncontrollably for over a second. We just wanted to say that our thoughts are with you at this sad, sad time" (cue sad music and/or wailing in the background.)
'Thank you for your thoughts'
"Now Edward, Ted, Mr Smith, before I talk to you further, I have to ask you some security questions. What is your date of birth?"

'Could you start by telling me who you are?'

"Yes Mr Jackson (my mother's re-married surname), I represent the Random Town Building Society and I work in their Bereavement Team (sob sob), what is your date of birth?"

'It's irrelevant, you don't know it, and how do I know you're who you say you are, you could be anyone calling from a number withheld phone line'

"We understand how upset you are, but please answer these questions for me"

<part of scene cut for brevity - we sort out security>

"Thank you, Mr Jackson. I understand that you want to close the account and for us to send you the proceeds, which are currently £104" (evidently my mother decided to join every Building Society under the sun when they were selling themselves off in the carpet bagging days)

'Yes'

"Ok, very sad, but we understand. Please could you now go online and fill out a form with just 178 irrelevant questions. Before you can do this, you will need to create a bereavement user account and create a password that contains a mix of capital letters, numbers, punctuation and hieroglyphics - after which we will send you a letter to your Mother's house confirming the secret code. Once you have done this please send us the original death certificate and original signed copies of her most recent phone, water and electricity bills and confirm her favourite colour and food."

......you get the picture.......tip for anyone dealing with a death......get at least 10 copies of the death certificate from the registrar, even the paper shop wants to see it before they will present you with the final bill!!!!!

6 April 2016

Yep, I'm on the train. And I'm in a different seat today - a family of tourists have stolen "my" seat.

What's my evidence to say they are tourists? Rucksacks which they hit people with rushing to the seat, having jumped the orderly British commuter queue, speaking Italian and looking at London guidebooks, and getting excited about whether Hatfield was a planned stop or not on this service (first time anyone has got excited about Hatfield in years).

So, tourists aside I am therefore sat opposite two of my classic pet hates and regular readers already know what's coming next. I just wish they read this, as tradition has it that we don't talk to each other on UK trains. Stop sniffing three times a minute woman! Blow your nose. Stick something up your nostrils. Take medication. But for pity's sake just stop sniffing so loudly!

And you! Isn't it obvious from my stares that I am not impressed with the effect that applying rouge is having to your cheeks? Besides it really doesn't match the purple streaks in your hair, or the chocolate brown lipstick that you just applied - or maybe that's the point - given that you have a blouse that has diagonal stripes and a skirt with horizontal stripes and leggings with dots, maybe you are going for the look at me - or maybe don't look at me?

And now I have a passenger next to me. He's also looking the make-up woman up and down. He's trying to do it surreptitiously (and failing), in the same way that you try to look at someone with an interesting feature.

And bingo. I like him. He has just pulled out a handkerchief and very deliberately blown his nose at the sniffing woman!!!!

Should I show him this???

9 April 2016
Before catching a lovely, on-time, hassle free train, I have to recount a story from breakfast in Firenze.

Yesterday a guest from NYC said to the restaurant manager: "I can only enjoy bacon and eggs with beans, could you please get some beans for tomorrow?"

Today, the manager has a huge smile on his face, there are eggs, bacon and Runner Beans!

4 May 2016
Girl age 3ish on the train opposite me: "but Dad this orange isn't working"

14 May 2016
Today the French achieved the impossible. They made British transport look good. Huge unmanaged crowds trying to leave a stadium set in an industrial area miles east of Lyon. A few trams. No extra buses. No trains. Quite ridiculous. It must have harmed the local economy. Instead of going into town to eat we are still miles away trying to choose between McDonald's and a local burger bar. Dreadful. At least we are a forgiving rugby crowd. I dare not think what it will be like when they play Euro16 football here.

2 June 2016
Great train experiences on my trip to and from Durham. On the way up - the train in front caught fire, everyone evacuated trackside, fire extinguished, back onboard and limped to next station. Hour delay. But nice old Virgin offered free Wi-Fi as compensation. At which point WIFI failed, as everyone in second class tried to link their 2 or 3 devices at exactly the same moment.
Every other train cancelled, due to overhead wires falling down, so standing room only for three hours. Well no, about twenty of us rebelled and stormed first class. Sadly no one inspected our tickets, and yet the staff did give us free tea or coffee, so our protest fell a bit flat. Only 45 minutes delay so way better on the way south than going up north.

Most train companies are poor at providing a service in the first place, and then when they make a mess of it, they are poor at making amends (and they never apologise in a meaningful or genuine way). SORRY, I meant ALL train companies in the UK.

Maybe John Lewis should be asked to run a line....... My sister isn't on, and never will be on, Facebook so I will have to tell the tale. Six weeks ago, she bought a new laptop, her old one expired, aged 8. She gets one with what she thinks is a huge memory, after all 32GB is 8 times more than her old one. Takes it home and installs MS Office.

At the weekend Windows 10 tried to update and the machine ran out of space. She only had 2MB of her own files on there!!!!!
So, she went back into JLP to ask what to do. They said that she shouldn't have been advised to buy it, and even though she had none of the packaging and it was over 28 days etc. they would happily copy her files onto a stick and give her all her money back. Jeez these guys are so good!! She then bought a 1TB machine (not much more cash as the prices have dropped). John Lewis Partnership. Thank you. Thank you.

28 June 2016
Feeling sad. I've just had a chat with a couple from Glasgow (aged early thirties I would guess) who were returning on the ferry after visiting their family on the Isle of Islay. They were worrying about the referendum result. I wrongly assumed they were Remain voters. But no, they had voted Leave as a protest but didn't want that result. They just wanted to poke the Government in the eye. I'd seen and heard of such people on social media but this was the first real couple trying to come to terms with what they had done that I have met. The only upside, from their perspective, was that Scotland would now become independent from the rest of the U.K. I wished them well. And then proceeded to use the EU funded facilities around

the port.

7 July 2016

Having commuted on the same train for several years I now know the best, the second best & etc. seats to be in, so that I can maximize my "Govia Great Northern traveling experience". They do not face the sun, are slightly wider, very near the exit, which in turn is close to the barriers on the arrivals platform, and they are just far enough away from doors and toilets and gangways to be knocked or gassed.

I also know most of the characters who will be competing with me for the seats. Today one of those characters had taken the optimum position on the platform for the best door to get to the best seat. The reason that "we" (I have no idea what others think, but I am sure they agree) all loathe her is that when she travels (Mon, Tues, and Thurs) she makes a huge song and dance about it. Yes, she has a ruck sack which randomly wipes-out the unsuspecting infrequent travellers. Yes, she has a big handbag. Yes, she spills everything everywhere. Yes, she does her make up whilst shouting into her phone as she tries to get the kids she has abandoned to go to school. Yes, she takes up two seats.

So today, having just read about the Chilcott enquiry cover-up thingy, I deployed shock and awe tactic number one.... The Blair charm offensive. And it worked! Standing right behind her I said "Morning!!" loudly to her for the first time ever.

She swung round, rucksack fell off her shoulder, handbag followed, she moved around to pick up the handbag whilst I got the rucksack and whilst she was doing that, I took pole position!!!!! Get in there.

Great start to the day.

17 July 2016

Conversations in queues at the festival for the shower block can be almost as interesting as those overheard on trains. Especially when you have a bunch of early-rising middle class facilities managers, all trying to devise a way in which the queue could be reduced, and debating the merits of unisex v single sex blocks, aware that the latter leaves trans people feeling left out. Quite surreal as well, being surrounded by people trying to catch Pokémon, and being told off for using their camera phones near the showers!

18 July 2016

I'm on a train from Brighton to London. It's 15 minutes late so far due to "congestion". This seems highly unlikely, since Southern have cancelled every other train! As everyone says, they clearly have no idea about how to run a service. My carriage is packed with German teenagers who are here to learn to speak English. They are going up to London to visit Parliament. So far, they have asked detailed questions about my views on Brexit and Theresa May, whilst taking notes. They are hoping to see her or Boris. These are not your average 14-year olds.

3 August 2016

I've just had to give up my seat and stand in the aisle away from the scene of all the action. No, not because there was a pregnant woman or an infirm old man, but because I had got the giggles and my political correctness meter had hit the red line.

So, what happened you ask? No, not that awkwardness when someone chooses to sit next to you when all the other seats are still empty. Or when you are hit by rucksacks and they don't apologise because they're unaware of the carnage behind them. No, not the lipstick slipping and going up the cheek, nor the coffee being spilt all down a lovely tie because the lid wasn't secure (ha! Schoolboy error).

Picture a nearly full set of seats. I'm on the end of a 2+2 and the set next to me is a 3+3 (this won't make any sense to those of you who travel First Class). In the line of three seats diagonally opposite me is a space.

In comes an exceptionally large man. Waist size must be pushing 60 inches? Regular travellers will know him on my line. He has a handlebar moustache just like in those old movies. And a tiny day sack with water and jangly keys in it.

"Is that free?"

Yes, he barges straight in and sits straight down! The guy on the left in the window seat gives a short sharp Yelp of pain and hurriedly tries to stand up, dropping his paper and phone. The woman on the aisle seat literally falls off into the aisle and spills her Diet Coke (I can't drink that stuff that early in the day).

No apology! He starts to read his paper!!!!! I'm so ashamed of my outburst of laughter that I help the woman get up and walk to where I am now, propping-up the door and giggling!

10 August 2016
Oh Bugger. That's all I could think to say when one of my closest friends told me they had cancer.

So now I am sitting on the train. Woozy from lack of sleep. Contemplating. This is one of those things in life that I can't just fix.

There's no funny punchline today. Instead a moment to reflect.

The good news is that our research teams keep finding better ways to treat different types of cancer. They learn how different chemicals and radio-therapies can reduce the spread, sometimes halt the disease.

But the mental strife can't be dealt with so simply. People are cut up, their loved ones torn apart. Fear, concern, worry are just the first ones that come to mind .... Fear of the unknown, concern about the side effects, worry about the outcome and lost time dealing with everything.

My thought for today though is this. This lovely person who's been affected can't tell everyone just yet. And it reminded me of the time I was HR Manager to a scientist who went through the horrors of cancer without telling anyone but close family and me. When the chemo was having its most devastating mental impact and she was still coming into work, no-one ever thought about whether she might have a health or a mental health issue, they just complained about her moodiness. One even asked me to investigate a possible drink problem.

So if you come up against someone who's a little moodier than usual, a bit snappy, a bit short with you, just step back a moment before giving them a hard time or complaining about them, they may be going through the wars back home, or they may be suffering silently - mentally or physically.

Love to you all. Ps she's still able to read this - it was 19 years ago - hope lives on.

16 August 2016
There's really something quite nice about a commuter train in the early morning in the middle of August. The sun is just over the horizon, it's warm and yet not too hot, the birds are singing, a cat stretches in a puddle of sunlight, the station roses start reopening for the day and the announcer explains that the delay today is excuse number 32, "lack of crew" - a completely understandable situation as they are probably on booked holidays and someone forgot to do the math's. Either that, or the temptation of a lie in on a lovely day, and the chance to not

be shouted at by angry passengers - who knows?

Anyway, we're now under steam (it's so noisy it might as well be) and my attempts at typing are punctuated by flashes of bright sunshine as the gaps between the trees allow the sunlight through. And I smile to myself knowing that Rebecca Leigh is safely back at home with her new baby Theo. As a transport aficionado she will probably be missing her commute, hence the name check to help make up for the loss.

I look up and see that carriage number 63064 is the noisy one, the smell of brake dust particularly strong today, and I know that Stephen Roughley will later be able to advise me where it was made and when it is due it's next service.

Why is it so nice to be traveling in August? BECAUSE I HAVE A SEAT! Yes, a real seat, with no one else on it and no one next to me. Luxury. And all because so many kind people have gone on holiday this week. Swapping delayed commuter trains for delayed planes and ferries. Well to those of you away at the moment - thank you. Enjoy your holiday as I enjoy my commute (and we are only the time it takes Usain Bolt to run 675 X 100 meters behind schedule which is actually rather good in itself).

8 September 2016
Today I spent 67 minutes on a tube train, travelling to Heathrow from Finsbury Park at 6.45am. Having stood in the middle of the aisle on boarding, I managed to grab a seat at Kings Cross as so many got off there, and proceeded to watch the people getting on and off.

The crowd on the train that I normally commute with are dressed for the office. Make up is applied, episodes of high-brow programmes viewed ostentatiously on iPads, Kindles flourished, and copies of Metro studied by those not playing games or writing train blogs on their smartphones.

The crowd on the tube featured a few of these, for sure, but at this time of the day (6am) the majority were clearly off to work on building projects, security roles, were catering assistants, or worked hospital shifts. Most just sat and slept, already knackered before the day started (or they had just come off shift?). Only one smartphone was being looked at. Regular changes on and off the tube.

Same rules as the train though. Avoid eye contact. Ignore the beggar walking down through the carriage, don't smile, just shuffle in and out at stations.

Except for one amazing young Asian guy. He got on at Kings Cross, could have nabbed a seat but instead gave way to a younger woman with a flourish of his hand and a bow. And then he started to sing! Such a beautiful voice that everyone woke up, looked, smiled and then .... Applauded!!!! No hat went around, no begging. He just bowed again and left at Holborn.

Lots of nods and smiles, then everyone closed their eyes and went back to normal.

What a lovely tube interlude, my day has started well :-)

9 September 2016
I'm struggling to believe how bad the internet is on the rail journey from Euston to Holyhead (for a wedding of two of my Glastonbudget friends, Neil Devenport and Caitlyn Da Costa). Firstly, the Virgin train Wi-Fi isn't. It's just a spinning cheese. Therefore, I'm reliant on something called gprs with occasional random bursts of E. Sounds like a cocktail of drugs.

So why is this important you ask? Well my good old faithful iPod shuffle is stuck on endlessly playing Autobahn. And it is doing my head in. I was innocently trying to use my iPhone to connect with my iTunes - but sadly in this modern digitally enhanced and moderated world, I need at least 3 Gs to have any chance, not one E. Anyhow - all is not lost. The guy next to me is playing Bob Dylan very loudly, and I can hear most of the (non-repeating) tracks - albeit it's a little too much treble. And Blonde on Blonde has some decent stuff on it.

Train running on time Paul Mez Merrick - get the beers in!!!!

11 September 2016
First the good news. Virgin Wi-Fi is working today. That will mean that I am saved from the agony of gprs with occasional E as we pass through unpronounceable towns along the North Wales coast.

Second the questionable news. Are seat reservations a good idea? All the seats in this carriage are reserved apparently, so moving may be problematic if someone is going to get on at Llanfairpwllgwyngyllgogerychwyrndrobwllllantysiliogogogoch.

But I am sat next to a group of lads who are speaking a strange language, and getting very excited about going on a trip to London. They are expressing their excitement by playing music through a blue tooth iSpeaker, whilst drinking lager with shots at, yes, 11am.

You have to have a reserved seat if you want a cheapie advance ticket, but this is going to be a big downside, especially as my head is still recovering from last night's wedding. More news will no doubt follow.

28 September 2016
I've now had the tenth person ask me if I am still doing my train blogs, so here goes with why the break. It's because I didn't want to bore you with my rants about Great Northern Abellio, they have been truly awful in the last few weeks with cancellations and serious delays on LITERALLY a daily basis.

We have had a train breakdown every other day, lack of train crew every day bar one and, more spectacularly a derailment and a lorry hitting a bridge to add to the usual suspects of signal failure, points failure and "following a slow train" (weird how they fail to spot this when organising the timetables).

Rant over. Today I am lucky enough to be sitting in a packed train. At long last my grey hair, hunched back and sad, resigned demeanour mean that the young man boarding at the same time as me didn't race to the one seat left, and deferred to me - or was that it was because he was my son James, with whom I am now commuting?!

Anyhow, I'm looking around for interesting observations. This is the "fast train" that I don't normally catch, so there are new people to study. There's a truly representative ethnic and gender mix, something HR peeps dream of, albeit no visible disability impairments - but my guess is that many are haunted by the black dog, the symbol for the very many who silently suffer from mental health problems.

Within sight I have 6 people fiddling with their phones, 4 readers of the Metro newspaper, 2 sleepers, 1 iPad watcher of a TV show, 1 nose picker and standing up I have 2 in a business conversation about loan rates, flapping their hands while all the others just stand looking at the floor. Not much meat for a blog there and unfortunately no make-up artists today (the slow train is best for that).

I contemplate instead. How lucky I am to have a job at a place I enjoy working at? How lucky that I still have most of my health, and a family that lets me take the only seat? What will I do today to encourage someone (maybe some people) to do something they weren't sure they could achieve (that's where I get my kicks)? And thoughts about a great friend of mine who's going through the horrors of cancer chemotherapy, and another who's finding out what it's like to be a proud mum for the first time. And finally, how lucky am I that the train is actually pulling into the station within a few minutes of its allotted arrival time!

10 October 2016

Today even the dreaded Starbucks is full. The majority are mildly to very annoyed commuters - but you can't tell, because they all have stiff upper lips. There are a few confused foreign students and some school kids who now know that all they have to say to their teacher, when late, is "trains" and everyone throws-up their arms and immediately understands.

Trains are really difficult things to organise. If they had been built with a straight track between stations, no points, and just a massive circle at each end to turn around with they would be fine. Actually, maybe not, they would still have to learn how to stop at stations, they would still breakdown and they would still run-out of staff every single day. But ours are even more complex. They have to navigate things called points and other mythical things called signals. These spend almost as much time not working as the train drivers themselves.

To make things more fun the customer information system (the tannoy) is only able to play pre-recorded messages which are telling us that the inclement weather (it's actually a beautiful morning) has made things dangerous: yep, so dangerous that the trains can't work. The other messages say that Great Northern Abellio are going to mess with the timetables (fewer trains, like Southern, to reduce their fines no doubt) and that anyone caught thieving will be prosecuted without delay. But what is there to steal? None of it works or has any value!

We learn that the excuse today is that a train broke down earlier at Drayton Park (can't blame it really, its retirement age keeps getting put back by the government - just like mine). They are trying to catch-up, but obviously the driver is now in the wrong place, and the replacement bus service that he's on is stuck in traffic that is "heavier than normal", due to all the people giving up on the trains no doubt.

Whilst I wait, I read the Daily Trump - the latest news about the great man. I bet he'd fix the trains - he'd grab them by the......

17 October 2016
Today I'm standing on the "fast" train and catching up on the latest news from across the pond. When I was working in North Carolina I witnessed a Presidential election and elections for Congress.

The State was always an interesting place to be, due to the large number of farmers and factory workers in the wider state, complimented by the concentration of pharmaceutical and high-end tech companies in RTP (Research Triangle Park). The big companies would often give campaign funds to both the Democrats and the Republicans, which always seemed strange, but was quite sensible I guess in terms of influence. I wonder if any are really funding Trump this time - it's certainly a double-edged sword! Speaking of which, please me know what 'trump' means to you:
1. The act of breaking wind, a fart
2. A significant card in a game of cards
3. To have superior power or authority over someone, or some group
4. To out-do
5. A lying racist misogynist
6. Super-hero in a wig

21 October 2016
The 05.50 is so different to the later one. Lots of sleeping people in various working uniforms. No noise, strong smell of cigarette smoke, and SEATs to sit on. Such a luxury - but no, I am not about to start this early normally.

Today is one of my days where I get to do something a bit different. Previously, I've spent a day on reception, and a day as a security officer, both brilliant. Both times I wore the uniform and was amazed how many people who knew me, looked straight through me, when I said good morning.

Today I'm joining the cleaning team. My rota includes windows, kitchens, toilets and then waste separation for recycling. The latter is something we want to lead on. We have managed to reduce by half, the amount of waste going to the tip in the past year - mostly by working on inter unit packaging - or asking suppliers to use reusable carriers rather than cardboard and plastic in simple terms. With food waste being bio-digested and everything else recycled we are now in a good place at 97% recovery. Onwards and upwards - environmental sustainability-just what I studied all those years ago when it was just a fledgling science.

26 October 2016
Traveling home on the late-night train after an excellent evening with some old Vernalis colleagues.

It's surprising how many young kids are on the train, not being adequately supervised by semi-pickled adults. I'm trying to work out how they have got into this state, and as I listen, I think it's that they have been out visiting worthy tourist sites all day, and then ended-up having an evening meal washed down with way too much booze.

At least this train is on time and relatively clean. Small mercies. At least we have trains. Unlike many of the places I have to work in Africa where the only forms of public transport feature minibuses packed with people, which only move when full both on the inside and the outside. Next trip is to Kenya, looking forward to it this time, as I will be traveling with a good friend and colleague who's on top of her game at the moment.

Tomorrow I get to see another of my favourites (I sound like Brucie at this point!), Sally-Louise Smith, can't wait.

1 November 2016

I'm on a South West train from Egham to Waterloo at the moment. It's surprisingly busy given the direction of travel, but then I discover the previous two trains had been cancelled. Same on every line then, except this one has toilets that work. A good idea for an old man who has been indulging in afternoon drinks. It's been both a sad and a happy day.

Sad to see off Doug Lipinski, who has left us whilst still too young. I was at school with him and played in a sixth form band with him called Yellow Pages, but given that he's a rock musician he has chosen to leave this world with lots of other musical celebrities - way too many in 2016.

Happy, because I had a chance to meet up with school friends Paul Cockrell and Martin Vermond. That gave us a great excuse to reminisce, and try to remember all the names of the six formers that we went to school with, and compare notes of what had become of them. Sad, happy, but thankful that I have known the gentle giant. RIP Lip.

9 November 2016

The rain is hammering down on the roof of carriage 77091 and more people than ever are staring at their phones. They're not playing games; they're reading BBC and Sky news apps. 2016 will be remembered, bigly, as the year when a shed load of celebrities died, just in time to avoid the carnage of Brexit

17 November 2016

People on trains do sometimes make me smile. It's not even 7pm and it's not even December, and we have a guy wondering down the corridor of the train trying to find the toilet because he is pissed (British pissed, not USA pissed) after his works Christmas (in the USA read Happy Holidays) lunch. CHRISTMAS

LUNCH ON 17/11 (11/17 in the USA), what is the world coming to?

Now this guy is seriously prepared for his visit to the toilet (Restroom in the US). He has already dropped his trousers (slacks) to his knees (no, not as in the fashion of young men, way beyond that) and has his hand holding his pants (briefs), ready to launch at a second's notice.

What he has failed to notice is that he has got on the slow train, which doesn't feature toilets (bathrooms). They are only on fast trains. What is the logic I hear my US friends ask, and I answer "nope", there is none. Board a slow train and hold it in, or a fast train and let it out.

Why all this reference to US language? Because several of you are surprised that I haven't yet Trumpeted my View in my train blog of the US election result. Well here goes. Reason is that Jim Peal has pretty much said it all. He's been using FB as a great cathartic opportunity, in the same way that I did over Brexit. We now know that disaffected folk have found their voice. They are no longer comfortable with the ruling class dictating their lives for them, they want to make a statement.

Be very interesting to see what happens now in France, Spain and Italy. I shudder to think. In the meantime, I'm preparing for Lord Alan Sugar, who runs The Apprentice UK, to put his hat in the ring to be king here.

22 November 2016
"We are sorry to announce...."

"We" is a computer-generated phrase maker that randomly jumbles excuses. It's the same "we" now as Govia Great Northern (surely they should drop the great?) as it was when it was Capital Connect ... and it's the same sad female computer voice.

What we listen out for is the next phrase. "Cancelled" is clinical and puts an end to any thoughts or concern. "Is running x minutes late" gives you hope. The deadly word is "delayed", which can mean literally anything! It's at this point that you listen out for the excuse of the day. "Ongoing signalling problems" is OK. It just means the driver has to phone ahead for permission to progress, so it's slow but sure. "A person being taken ill" is generally bad news. There's a long wait and the line is blocked, so all following trains are delayed - but it's hard to blame the train operator except on those rare days (i.e. Every day) when people are rammed in like sardines and get overcome.

"Due to a broken-down train". Mmmm. Blocked track? Can be a major headache. "Due to no driver being available". Really this is rubbish. We've been hearing this for ten months now. It is time to hire some drivers guys.... that's a fairly fundamental 101 training (get it) course that all operators should attend. We need track, trains and drivers. Doh!!!

And finally, "Inclement weather" is just laughable. They have been running trains for more than a hundred years. Come on guys. It's the U.K. It rains sometimes!

When commuting, the other joy is the announcement that confirms the train is arriving at the station but "is formed of four coaches". Arrrrrrrggggghhhhhhh! It's full and standing only with 8, can you therefore imagine 4?! But clearly no apology is needed. The inference is that "you are lucky we managed to find 4 coaches that work in the rain".

26 November 2016
Headlines on the free paper as I travel in to town: RIP Fidel Castro. Seems fitting to go in 2016 with everyone else.

7 December 2016 Mild overnight. Leaves have all blown away. Track is not slippery. Signals are behaving. Drivers are not sick. End result: train arrives early and then departs before it's due time (yes, my watch is radio controlled and accurate to milliseconds!). A new insult. Given that this service has departed between 3 and 10 minutes late every day for months and the only apology has been on behalf of the weather or illness Gods, it doesn't feel great.

But it does give me a chance to get a seat on the slow train and watch a new set of commuters from my seat. So not all bad then!
I have 8 in my eye line. All on their phones. I think 5 are playing games by the look of their hand movements. Two are typing messages and the last one is probably watching a video. No make-up artists. No eaters. No drinkers. This is a serious commute. But that's a tad boring to train blog readers who need more. And you're all thinking, why is he writing this without much to say?

Well, it's because of the guy who has chosen to stand by the door. There are lots of seats still, by the way. He is in a dark suit, with what was once a white shirt and his tie is completely open hanging around his neck. His hair is all over the place. He has sunglasses on and it's still dark outside. And I'm wondering whether he will make it all the way to London without emptying the contents of his stomach.

I am so tempted to chat to him and find out. My theory, based on the creases in his trousers and jacket, beer looking stains on his shirt, a thick brown stain on his jacket sleeve and what looks like chutney in his ear, is that he is one of the first Christmas (US friends = Happy Holidays) party semi casualties that didn't make it home last night and is now learning about the treats of the Great Northern Abellio FCKU railway company.

But here's the final intrigue. The train started at my station. But he was already on it. So where did he start, and where will he end his journey?

12 December 2016

Completely different commute this morning via a visit to Denham. Made me realise how awful it would be if I was still driving around the M25 to Stockley Park. One jam after another, and lots of aggressive drivers weaving and going nowhere fast. All because of a bit of fog and drizzle.

Anyhow, the train part of the journey is also interesting. £6 for the car park and then breakfast whilst I waited for the train.

"Morning, Bacon roll please" (there being huge advertising boards saying how delicious they were). "Sorry, out of them" Sausage in a bap? "No, sorry" Now before you worry about another cheese shop sketch by Monty Python, I just picked up a croissant and was done with. "And a black Americano please." Ages later, having refilled the dispenser with coffee and then hand-ground each nut "you did say latte, didn't you?"

Next came paying for it. "My till doesn't work and my phone battery has died, can you work out the cost on your phone please?" I was almost speechless, but I said how much it was (2.20 plus 1.70) "£3.90" and handed over a fiver.

"But can you check it on your phone and show me?"

All good fun. Now on the train. Train is on time and I have a seat. Small mercies. And before you ask, the black Americano is fine.

18 December 2016

After years of being teased about my inability to wrap presents, I have really tried hard this year. And failed again. I think it's because it's 2016. Next year can't be anything but better.

41

(Except for the trains, which are preparing a new winter schedule - and we know what that means!). Happy Christmas Everyone!

30 January 2017

Today I'm travelling up to Birmingham on a Midland train, which is almost running to schedule. I was very excited to have bought a First-Class ticket for £16, until I got on board and realised that the seat had to be fought for and that people are standing, and that there are no facilities and that it stops everywhere! It's a proper tour of the south and East Midlands.

1 February 2017

Yes, I have a seat, but Wi-Fi is a no-go on this west coast Virgin service back to London. My speech went really well, even though it was at the end of two days of conferencing, with a lovely lady standing up to ask this question "did you know that yours was the best talk I have attended in two days?" NOT one to ever be humble I thought I should post this here! And no mention of wellbeing, but lots on nudging change along with pilot schemes and putting yourself in the shoes of those who work in all the different roles your organisation has. I'm still smiling.

16 February 2017

First train update in a little while. Brought on by the light entertainment division of Ungreat Abellio Northern Franchise Ltd (Ltd stands for limited trains and drivers).

The 06.52 closes its doors a full minute early. No complaint. The rules say it can. My fault for not being there on time. The 07.03 is, of course, cancelled "due to over-running engineering works". These haven't affected other trains so we are all somewhat confused.

The 07.15 slow to Moorgate is the answer. And it's sitting there on platform 4. We get on. We are asked to get off as this train is going to the sidings. We stand around in the cold as everyone is removed. It is now announced that the 07.15 is delayed.

Delayed thankfully by all of 25 seconds, something of a record for a delayed train, and thus making it one of the most on-time delayed trains ever on this line. And yes, you have guessed it: it's the very train we all had to get off that we are now getting back onto! And it's going to be rather full as we go down the line picking up people who couldn't get on the cancelled train.

But there is a silver lining. The driver is not a chatty man. Sometimes early in the morning it's difficult to cope as they burble on!

22 February 2017
Today I'm on the 09.41 (which has turned into the 09.46 by the miracle of the train being in the wrong place due to earlier signal failure) after a run in with the dentist - who felt that it would be fun to replace an old filling - fun for him that is. I'm a dribbling wreck as a consequence and now hooked on anaesthetics.

It's different to my normal train - it's the first one that is off peak. Peak is defined as before 09.30. And yet it's pretty full. Maybe filled by sensible people with flexi hours that only have to pay half the normal fare? (Fare is such a wrong word for something that is so unfair).

The most interesting fellow sufferer (sorry, passenger) is an elderly Chinese businessman making a lengthy mobile call. He is moving between English and Chinese mid-sentence, so I'm only getting half the story. And no, I am not eavesdropping, I am being forced to hear this due to the simple fact that his personal volume control is defective.

Anyhow, it seems that his son is studying here in the U.K. and is in a spot of bother, hence the train journey that has somehow brought him here from Stansted. And I think money is involved. I'm just hoping that he doesn't get off at Hatfield for the University as this is all quite interesting!

27 February 2017
Sometimes life is just full of coincidences, but this morning is particularly special. Opposite, and across from me, a young man has just eaten his breakfast on the train. A bagel (simple cream cheese I think), followed by a bar of chocolate. Yes, chocolate for breakfast. And why not, it's no worse than a hot chocolate, or if you accidentally end up in Starbucks it's probably less sugar than one of their winter specials, and the caffeine will help him wake-up ready for work. I wanted to ask what the cocoa percentage was.

Why the coincidence? Because we had the honour of spending the evening with Ruzica Ru Crnojacki Micanovic (better known as Ru) and Vlad last night to pick up a year's supply of clothing and boots and other essentials to take to their daughter in New Zealand.

After an amazingly light and tasty cheese flan, we were treated to a choice of chocolate and here I do need your thoughts. We started with Orange dark chocolate, then pistachio. Both rather good, then we worked our way from 60% to 70% to 80% to 90% cocoa in a kind of wine tasting way.

For me 90% is just too bitter, but that is just the first taste, after it lingers in the mouth it leaves a very satisfying flavour, more so than the lower percentages. I think the young man's was probably 50%, he's missing out on a treat!

21 March 2017
Thank you to so many of you who have messaged me to check that I'm OK. I hadn't realised how much you missed my train blog. Today's commute was a lovely surprise after a few weeks away to visit my son in the New World. I arrived at Kings Cross

to discover that the new double decker trains to Paddington are air conditioned and run twice as often and twice as fast. Totally brilliant! Just a shame I'm in Sydney in Australia!

22 March 2017

This train blog features the train, maybe funicular, that travels up the side of the mountain alongside Hong Kong. A small town on the south coast of China that is renowned for high rise buildings and aerial walkways and ferries between the islands rather than trains and trams. I loved the orderly queues, the general cleanliness of the area and the sparkling nature of the train carriage itself, something that you don't see in the London version of Kings Cross every day. The trip was delayed by a full minute due to a safety concern (a tourist leaning on the door) and the staff apologised profusely. In London they only apologise when they are ten minutes late.

Inside the car again, so very clean. No chewing gum in sight, no spilt drinks or empty McDonalds bags. Why? Because (a) no one would dream of dropping litter and (b) if they did so accidentally a staff member would mysteriously appear from nowhere and give it back to them before they could walk ten yards.

I really enjoyed my first trip to HK. It lived-up to the hype, and was a fascinating mix of cultures, technologies, people, styles .... albeit dominated by money and wealth. The haves have a much better time than the have-nots.

23 March 2017

Trains in New Zealand are hard to come by. Mostly used for hauling freight, there are a small number of passenger services, but you really do need to rely on the InterCity buses and aeroplanes, or hire a car/mobile home to get around, especially after earthquakes have had an impact, which is the only downside of what otherwise is a beautiful country to visit.

And by beautiful, I mean amazing. I have so many photos that it will be a while before I can sort out the best ones to try and show a hint of the majesty of this living geology lesson. Remember 'U' shaped glacial valleys from your Geography lessons? Yep, you can start at the top of one, and walk down and see hanging valleys en-route. Then there's the simple fact that everyone we met wanted to help ensure that we were having a great time, no jobs-worth mentality that we came across. Even moving outside some of the tourist routes and areas, and going off into small towns we found the same, albeit often people with little or no money, but proud.

I can see why people come here and want to stay. It's miles away from the madness of Trump and Brexit and North Korea, but I wonder if I could cope with occasional visits to the Islands from Bieber and Adele (yep both were there when we were) and a rugby team that just go around winning everything?

2 April 2017

Bit of a shock this morning. A brand, spanking-new train. It's a real quandary that it puts me in. What is there to blog about? Hopefully Stephen Roughley can look at the identifier number and let me know where it was built. Maybe it's not new and just refurbished?

Amazing these days that so much of the human body can be refurbished. I have two friends who have recently undergone elective heart surgery and a favourite Aunt who has been given another chance with stent technology. Three others (yep they are coming in threes) are being rebuilt with surgery following breast cancer treatment. All of these things just weren't available when close members of my family were affected earlier in my life.

But where is the line to be drawn? Should a line be drawn? Could we get to the point where someone has tech eyes, ears and speech and full mobility exoskeletons and just the brain distinguishes them from a robot. Actually, we are already there, it's just cumbersome and not refined yet.

Thoughts? 1 Excited. 2 Scared. Or 3, hey Ted I've just woken up, it's Monday morning for goodness sake!

4 April 2017

Am I a magnet for people with colds? I sat down in a nearly empty carriage on the train in this morning, and now we are approaching London I have sneezers to the left of me, and sneezers to the right, here I am stuck in the middle. Also front and back, but I'm not sure which song that references.

Some have good habits. They have a hankie (spellcheck came up as Jackie???) ready and seem to contain their ejections. But to the left we have a full-on let it all out woman, who I'm thinking about speaking to (I've tried glaring). The trouble is that with this sunlight inflicted on us by the introduction of daylight-saving hours, I am forced to watch the spray circle round towards me!

I've thought very positively about this and declared in my head that there is nothing contagious. Surely, it's just hay fever kicking in?

7 April 2017

Utterly brilliant today. 07.03 cancelled obviously. We get on to the 07.15.

Driver "please calmly, but quickly, get off the train, no need to panic". Staff on platform SCREAMING "get away from here NOW, move, move, move, it's going to blow!"

Some passengers run-up and over the bridge whilst others are herded to the end of the platform, whilst one guard gets increasingly scary and the other tries to calm things down.

I was obviously a rebel and went over the bridge to catch the 07.27. The other train hasn't blown-up yet, but it is smoking!!!!

This will be the best reason for a delay reclaim yet.

8 April 2017

Arrived at the station only to be told that the train is delayed in arriving. But it is sat there at the station, next to Platform 4, so it clearly isn't.

Next, we are told that we are awaiting a driver. Next, we are told there are signalling problems. Next, we are told the train will go direct to Kings Cross, without stopping. Next, we are told it was cancelled. Normal service has been resumed.

What I am doing these days is claiming for every journey that I am delayed by 15 minutes or more. I hate the thought that they should benefit from my misery as they (the operator) get a load of cash from the track operators every time signalling is an issue. I delight in the thought that my claim - which is only tiny and may get me £7-ish back will cost them £30-Ish to process. Small things keep this small mind ticking. Sorry to my mentee, who is the real loser in this, as I am at least 30 mins behind schedule.

Good Friday April 2017
Today I'm travelling on the enhanced Saturday service train to London on a Friday and yep, it's delayed. The good news is that I will still make it in time to the Royal Albert Hall where I'm taking my little sister to see Handel's Messiah - it has been sung every Good Friday there since 1876 - about the date when the last train arrived on schedule.

19 April 2017
"Good morning and welcome to this late running Kings Cross service calling at...." and yet it's only a minute late, normally that's considered well within the bounds of tolerable service levels (actually up to 14 minutes late is considered on time by our franchisees). The train was delayed due to "electrical

problems". Given that it's a newish train I assume that's with the power supply rather than the train itself, but hold on, the excuse given to the people getting on at the next station is that there were signalling problems. Well maybe the signals didn't have enough electricity to be bothered to start-up?

In the meantime, my morning Metro newspaper has actually heard about the election. Sometimes I think it is sent to print so early the previous day that most actual news (as opposed to celebrity gossip and pictures of Trump doing weird things) gets lost, albeit they clearly have a sports writer who works up until 6pm.

So, let the super accurate pollsters begin their poisonous job of telling us with absolute certainty that the election will go a particular way, to be out-witted by the people again .... although this time there doesn't actually seem to be any opposition in England and Wales - unless Nicola runs SNP candidates on a pro EU ticket down here?

I'm saddened that Corbyn has not turned into any kind of leader and is still fighting his own team. I'm saddened that most people haven't a clue who the LibDem leader is (but there are no Millennials voting for them anyway after having their education messed up by Clegg), and I'm not sorry that nobody knows who the UKIP leader of the day is - least of all the UKIPers themselves.

26 April 2017 Train blogs can feel a bit trivial in the face of life-changing and life-threatening illnesses and diseases at home, whilst elections rage in Europe and the US flexes its nuclear muscle in Afghanistan, Syria and North Korea.

And yet the mocking of a train company for blaming the track, the weather, the signals and even its own drivers for the lateness of a single short journey, allows me to joke about some things, comment about weird people applying their make-up badly or being drunk at 7am.

So, why did I start this by mentioning illnesses? I guess it is simply that having worked in pharma, biotech, a major health funding agency, and now a major health charity throughout my life, I am still knocked back by the simple fact that when it comes to an individual dealing with something like a life threatening aggressive cancer, or a debilitating mental illness which the medicines won't help, there is so little anyone can practically do apart from try to offer support to the person and their loved ones.

I try not to preach sermons in my blogs, but there is a clear thing here. It's about living life in the moment, enjoying the short time you have on this planet, fighting stuff when you have the passion, and remembering that there is always someone around you that needs your love and support more than you realise..... and that is especially true for those with a mental illness that isn't as blatantly obvious as a physical illness.

One or two of you reading this will think I am talking about you. I am. I am talking about everyone.

10 May 2017
For those of you awaiting my next train blog, there is a real resonance about being at Swindon Station, the once proud home of GWR.

Just had a catch up with some of my favourite people. Some reminiscing about the good times at the MRC and catching up on the gossip.

Regarding trains, well I have a seat. I'm facing backwards, but I have a seat. It seems relatively clean, but I'd forgotten how heavy and old fashioned the doors are on this line, the art of leaning out the window at the station whilst juggling bags and drinks.

Nice thing - I tried to give a tip to the two ladies at the cafe on the station after they had made me a flat white. They refused. I countered. They eventually let me put the money in the local hospice charity box, even though they didn't know me and then told me very proudly how much they raised in the past month. They were both lovely, but the coffee was basically a milky white. Not even vaguely a flat white. Hey ho.

25 May 2017
This morning, after a trouble free, on-time train service, I arrived at Kings Cross to be greeted by the "Meet the Manager" team of Ungreat Northern Rail and franchise partners.

First person I met turned out to be from the support agency that set up the event. The second was someone who I think might be in training to become a manager (because he had all the buzz words to hand). Neither could deal with my concerns about the lack of drivers and strange policy related to Moorgate (train length means it can't be used on diversion from Kings Cross etc).
The fun came when I turned away and walked over to the ticket machine (the new ones won't let you buy the return half of a carnet from your home station) to buy my carnet. A member of the barrier crew smiled and I said hi. And he said "I wish they'd bother to meet their own staff; we can see the problems and half the time we have the answers, and often they could save money".

A good lesson for my day at work coming up....

1 June 2017
Classic entertainment on the train today. Male, mid-twenties, designer beard, sharp suit, trainers on feet and black suede shoes in hand joins us at Hatfield, and immediately starts

making loud phone calls.

The first to a recruiter. Snippets include: "no mate, just started, loving it, call me again in a few weeks, coz if they don't sort the bonus then I'm out"; "Commutes better, I can call me mates on the way in"; and "I'm on 25 big Gs basic so it's all about the commission and I'm good for that".

Then to a friend "haven't spoken to you for days.......well yeah alright since yesterday", "you know I got home about 2am after I dropped you off, well yeah had to get up at 6am to do some ironing, then I had some toast and a coffee and then I put some jumpers in the communal drier - hope they don't steal my £50 jumper".

Then to the next friend "Hi, thought I'd call and make your day, sorry we're going into tunnels soon so might get cut off, wanted to tell you about me new job.....sorry redialled.... yeah lovin' it, yeah, great boss and great place and they let me make decisions but I dunno if I'll get a bonus so I might leave.... yeah sorry going to have cut you off now, gotta order me a Tesco food drop for tonight".

Can you imagine the dread that would surge through your body if you had a friend who called you at 7.15am to talk such nonsense? Every word was about self. Not one question, or enquiry, about how the friend was doing. Entirely wrapped-up in his own world.

Cue older bloke behind me, in a very plummy voice, "what a Tosser" followed by chuckles all around as people suddenly raised their newspapers over their faces. In my case this led to more chuckling as I read the memes #wheresmay after 'She' chose to avoid the TV debate.

11 June 2017
Thoughts composed on a train.

I first met Sally-Louise Smith in the year 2000. She was a key member of the HR team that I was responsible for at Glaxo. She had just left BA, and brought all sorts of ideas and a different way of working, with special emphasis on real customer care. Given that we were hiring lots of programmers at the time, and going through a major change programme, she really stood out - and not just because of her blonde hair and red lipstick - more because of her ability to help people find their best - Sally was the Queen of Productivity, encouraging and developing people, getting them to push themselves that little bit further.

I moved away from GSK and then bumped into her again when she landed a job a few years later at RCUK. We had a coffee (I know, not the Sally you all know), lunch, then we ended up on a working group and before you know it, we were making research council music together!

It wasn't long before an opportunity came up to re-hire Sally, first into a transition project manager role and then a few months later as my Deputy HR Director.

In that role Sally was totally amazing. She quickly made friends with so many people, she took control of numerous tough projects, she nurtured and guided many junior team members and she just made stuff happen without drama, without tears, just an amazing smile and motivating words.

By now Sally and I had moved on from coffees and onto "the odd glass of Malbec" - much needed with the workload of the university transfers. It was on one of those evenings that we dreamt up the people strategy and Sally's desire to take a lead role in Wellbeing, something that the MRC became very well known for.

When I moved on, it was Sally who took up the role of HR Director at the MRC, and from all accounts she took the role up a notch to a higher level, building a brilliant working relationship with The team.

Sally found Malc during this time and I have to say that she could not have been happier. A truly wonderful man and superb husband to be. She found supreme happiness, she was one of the hardest working and most successful HR people I have ever known, and leaves a huge gap in many lives. She was one of those rare people in life who people spoke well and highly of when she was alive. And then during her illness she astounded us with her courage and desire to keep going right up to the last minute. I really do feel that I am one lucky man, to have had the opportunity to both work with her and to be a friend outside work.

Love you Sally. Xxxxx

12 June 2017
Wow, the age of the FB video is now definitely upon us. I've just counted 18 posts in a row from friends and advertisers (equal mix) that are video format or gifs before hitting the first static photo post. And the other thing? All are from "my" generation. Next two generations down have clearly abandoned FB in favour of things like Instagram and Snapchat and Peach and the mid generation on Twitter.

Loving how fast this world is moving. Shame the PM isn't keeping up and has just selected the same old losers for her cabinet un-shuffle - how on earth did we end up with a conservative coalition of chaos with the DUP and the likes of Gove, BoJo and Hunt in serious roles? The invite to May's leaving party at the end of the month currently circulating on all forms of social media at least got me smiling again, almost as good as the Osbourne Dead Woman Walking quote.

So many distractions happening at the moment, how can I possibly focus on what other passengers are doing on the train right now? Oh! Apart from that woman who is doing her make up on the way home this time?! And clearly is unmoved by the absolute look of disdain from the older woman next to her ...... I feel a video coming on!!!!

1 September 2017
So, what's it been like commuting during the summer? Seats on the way in to London - something that will disappear next week - have been a real luxury which I have thoroughly enjoyed. But seats on the way back haven't always been so easy to find, as parents fill them with tired kids who have been dragged around the tourist attractions, and tourists fill spaces with their bags as they push further out of high season to get cheaper hotels and lodgings.

Fewer funny incidents. Those commuting are either recovering from a holiday, or anticipating one, and don't do strange things when squeezed out of their normal seat - because they still have a choice of which seat to take.

Trains still have problems of course. On rare sunny days they get way too hot sitting in the sidings, and feel like cookers when you walk into them on the journey home. That's when they can close their doors - the brand-new trains have been failing because the door sensors are too sensitive (not something you could say about the couple of electricians boasting about their day with an apprentice in the seats to my left side!).

And, of course, our train non-operator has been caught out by very difficult circumstances. "The 19.03 has been cancelled due to driver shortages". Yep they unexpectedly wanted to take a summer holiday, and no-one had planned for this weird behaviour.

Of course we have also had overheated points, sticky signals, mice eroded cabling and rather more trespassers on the tracks than I had expected, but the train operators just say sorry and explain about delay repay schemes which require a lot of form filling, and even then are contested (I've made 12 claims and had success with 9; the others I should have known to change at Finsbury Park and travel back in time to catch the earlier train, apparently, and I honestly couldn't be bothered to make an appeal to the Ombudsman).

So summer is over and schools are back and I will be standing again next week ...... roll on the half term holiday!!!!

1 September 2017

In days gone by, trains and buses weren't considered an environmentally sustainable way to travel. With so few cars around they were called essential public transport! The enclosed story reminds me of this big switch - the road where I used to play cricket is no longer a cricket pitch, it's a densely packed car park.

My Dad died when I was 14 years old. The next couple of years were spent in admin mode, trying to be the man of the house and coming to terms with a strange world which struggled with single parent families (the divorce rate rise seems to be linked to the increase in multi car ownership!), but I look back now and realise a good portion of confidence was also lost.

A good friend convinced me to try out Venture Scouts. I hadn't been a cub or a scout or, indeed, a brownie, so I had assumed it was impossible. But no, I attended a first meeting and loved it from the word go. Little did I know that I was a part of something quite amazing.

I was part of the first ever mixed VSU in the UK and, according to a man who knows these things (Austen Cordasco), it was also the first mixed unit in the world, and it was Peter Bates who had to fight his way through both the hierarchy of the scout and the guide movements at that time to make it possible.

But it doesn't end there. The reason that Peter is special is the way that he ran the unit. He didn't dictate what would be done week by week, instead he had a committee of young people making those calls, up to and including planning walking and hiking and rock climbing and barge and sailing boats and caving etc. weekends away all over the UK.

As a direct consequence of Peter's leadership style, I took on responsibilities, learned how to manage expeditions (the biggest probably being the Plainsman Hike) and grew in confidence. So, I owe a lot of my positive early days to Peter.

And Saturday night was a great way to celebrate the unit and to catch up with Peter. Now back to my journey (no weird people so far and I have a seat!).

8 September 2017
Thank goodness I got up for the early train, given that the 07.03 and several others are cancelled, again, because our glorious train company hasn't planned for staff taking holidays. At least they didn't lose the train this time!

I also have a seat. I guess because it's a Friday and so many office people work from home. BUT I can't nod off. Behind me is an angry typist. He is seriously bashing the hell out of the keyboard of his laptop. Almost to the point where I was going to see if I could record the evidence! As in wow! Maybe he hates his current laptop and is trying to break it so that his works IT team will have to replace it?

Reminds me of the time when the original Glaxo tried to change its sales reps car policy from a new car every 18 months to one every two years. The reps simply visited dodgy crime areas and made sure they were stolen at.... 18 months.

Which also reminds me of the biscuit factory where management tried to reduce the number of fag (US - smoke) breaks. The guys on the line simply threw a small screw or bolt into the magnetic scanner, the line shut down whilst Q&A were called and they all had a ciggie!

Maybe the train drivers have found a way to......

20 September 2017
Today's train journey is through the mountains as I make my way from Salzburg to München. The train is very clean. The ticket inspector speaks at least 4 languages (German, English, French and Japanese). She needs the latter as there are some tourists taking photos out of the window every minute...... oooh look a cow (maybe my translation is not so good, but I'm pretty sure that's what they got very excited by).

The train is on time. At the last stop we left a latecomer behind. The train is, however, way too warm. No windows that you can open and the aircon has either failed or isn't on. But I know you read this blog for the people stories, not the Ted train scoring system (TTSS).

And I am amazed. There is a group of very loud Austrian teenage girls. As in badly behaved and rude to their elders and, well, very noisy. With my iPod in my ears I can still hear the shouts. And sadly, the inspector can't resolve it, even with her grasp of so many languages. The current fun is that they all have overly large skirts and are taking it in turns to pull them over their heads whilst shouting something suspiciously like "Achtung!" which is really annoying an older lady near me.

31 October 2017
After an interesting visit to Durban, South Africa (for "interesting" read "it's definitely not a holiday destination"), to

see the work on TB and AIDs being undertaken by AHRI (the African Health Research Institute), I'm now back enjoying the pleasures of GNUK railways. Yesterday was not good. Although the incident at Hatfield (someone hit by a train we believe), was not the responsibility of the Rail companies, their dreadful communications for the next two hours were. It became very clear that the people in the GNUK social media room had no clue about what was happening, nor about the geography of the area. They were also lazy, they started by cutting and pasting from the Virgin Rail feed "incident in the Stevenage area". Next, they said there was an incident in Hitchin and then, only later, in Hatfield.

At one point, trains north of Hitchin were affected due to the incident there. Lol. No, they weren't. Those trains were still stuck at Potters Bar.

Worse, they relied on Rail apps to suggest things like "it looks like the 08.42 is still running". As if!!!!

Today reminded me of Airplane the movie. (For younger readers this is a must see - it's free to view on most systems these days). In that movie the plane kept changing gates. Today we started on platform 3. We're sent to 2. Then sent to 1. Then sent back to 2.

The staff at the station can only shrug. They are given no information and just have to do their best.

6 November 2017

Last Monday we had a suicide on our rail line at Hatfield. Today another at Ally Pally.

So sad for the people involved and their friends and family. That they have got to this point. And not found a way out.

Even worse for the train drivers and the emergency services who have to deal with it. I really do feel for them. How do you drive a train again, knowing this might happen again?

And on the other side of the coin you have our train operator. Who I have nothing but contempt for.

Each time there is an incident (last week included two lots of overhead cables coming down, and a lorry ramming a bridge, as well as three broken down trains) they leave their staff in the dark. So, the staff do their best.

The tweeters tweet nonsense based on electronic train boards that bear no relationship to reality, and the Station staff tell you one story, which the drivers then challenge by offering a different story.

Please could someone in a senior position at Great Northern please stand up and be counted and start getting reliable communications out? Surely there is now a play book that covers each type of incident?

It really is pathetic to keep being referred to the delay repay scheme as if that is the end of it. We are losing hours of our time to your incompetence.

Grant Shapps MP apologises on their behalf, and promises to take action. But, of course, he is conflicted as a supporter of privatisation. Sad days.

19 November 2017
Daniel Kitson mentioned trains in his two-hour monologue without a break at the Roundhouse in Camden last night (see what I did there?). He talked about a time when he tried to fight the passenger next to him for the right to put a part of his elbow on the arm rest that divided the two seats. This is something that I have had in theatres and cinemas for years, so it struck a chord. The upshot is that he lost, but she overbalanced having applied so much pressure. At which point they both apologised to each other, and then never touched the

arm rest for the rest of the journey!

I've had something similar on the train. But with a man who sat next to me and insisted on splaying his legs wide open so that he encroached on my space. This now has a term for the uninitiated: manspreading. Women rarely do it apparently, having been trained as teenagers to keep their legs close together for all sorts of different reasons. So, what did I do - having failed to push back and feeling hemmed in? Women you can learn something here! I started applying my make-up, deliberately dropped my blusher, had to bend down to pick it up. His legs had to be retracted. I sat up and extended my legs as I did so. Battle won! Territory gained! (For blusher read anything that you can drop that doesn't end-up in an expensive bill, e.g. a phone). Happy Journeys everyone!

23 November 2017

What better way to start your Day, than with a bit of laughter? Having sat at a red light for a while on the train, across the intercom come the priceless words, said with childish incredulity "I can see a train coming." The people around me all had the same reaction and the banter was great. Clear pleasure that our driver can actually identify other trains, the fabulous news that other trains were actually moving, thanks that he wanted to share this joyous news (other drivers just don't give you any such information - indeed in all my years of train commuting I don't think that a driver has ever told us when he has seen another train before).

Early in the morning and a smile does you good. Especially when it's still dark outside, the rain has started and the winds haven't yet fully died down.

Speaking of winds, if I were the Council leaf collection sub-contractor I'd be out there today. All those little eddies and whirl pools have collected all the loose leaves into neat piles or concentrated drifts all over town. Good job most of the leaves have fallen, if they had still been full of leaves then a few trees would have lost branches last night.

4 December 2017

We're currently a full carriage of commuters travelling about 60mph towards London. And, as tradition has it, we are a good few minutes behind our schedule.

In the UK, train timetables are either fake news or a fiction. It really is up to the reader to try and discern whether there is any truth in them whatsoever.

The signallers need to look after our safety, and so make us stop for long periods in the only part of the countryside where there is no mobile signal.

The drivers are so thinly stretched, and unfortunately reliant on other trains to get them to where they need to drive their trains from, and so are often late.

The station staff who are on pension schemes are being "voluntarily" retired early, and replaced by apprentices who do their best in a bewildering non-system.

And the "communicators" in the twitter and web HQ are taught to answer every enquiry with the question "where are you trying to get to" and then to move on to the next customer quickly before they have to make up an answer. Although if forced they will always helpfully tell you that you that your tickets are valid on local bus services and fictitious trains from other providers, that just happen to be miles away from where you are. Their knowledge of geography leads them to believe that Hitchin and Hatfield are next door to each other, and that St Albans is a short bus ride away. Lol.

So, Trump didn't invent fake news. Govia Great Northern Non-Railway (sister of Southern) did!

6 December 2017
I have a seat! But the really good news is that normal service has been resumed after overhead cable problems, ahem, again, in the Stevenage area meant that the trains were totally screwed up last night. Most people are standing, but that's normal. They are also celebrating the above inflation fare rises coming in January.

My son James had a brilliant response from the poor station staff that had just come on duty at 11pm at the height of the 6 hour problems last night and confirmed that he had been given no information about what was happening, the reason for a train not moving at Finsbury was because the driver was out of place. He was stuck at Kings Cross and there were no trains to take him to Finsbury Park, the barrier guy just shook his head when asked why the driver couldn't either take the tube, a bus, a taxi or even walk?

Difficult to make these stories up (so I don't).

I'm looking forward to the break coming up, when I won't have to rely on Govia to transport me to work.

16 December 2017
No trains, just selling a car and some info for anyone thinking about using webuyanycar dot com, one of the fastest growing companies who have cornered the market and removed the hassle of car selling (their words). They are the people who give you an instant quote online and then they don't haggle, they are nice, like Philip Schofield, and they make an appointment and give your money instantly. That's the adverts sorted.

The reality is that you get an attractive price online, close to Parker's Guide price. Tick. They don't come to your house; you visit them in a rented Regus office. There is no mechanic, instead it's a salesman, a good one, who has phoned you twice to check that you're coming, and he takes you through lots of paperwork in a warm office whilst chatting about you, and he has great listening skills.

The trip to see the car is the least amount of time of the whole deal. Checks the car starts up and runs at idle, checks the front electric windows are working. Checks there is a spare tire and parcel shelf. Then counts all the little dinks and paintwork defects. Mutters about every little blemish (the plumber school of training, "ooh I don't like the look of that one."

Then it's back to the office and every little scratch is entered. The original internet offer was 2655. Less all the scratches it's now 1895.

I say that I'd been warned about this, but hadn't realised how bad the revised offer would be, and that, thanks, I would sell privately and get going before wasting his time any more.

At which point he declares that he is a manager, and therefore he has some room to allow for discretion and suggests we sit back down. More muttering.

After several coats being done up and then undone, we arrive at 2239. I was so pleased that there was no haggling needed! But the story doesn't end there. As you go to sign the paperwork (now an hour after arriving), you discover that there is an admin fee of £50, not previously mentioned, and that if you want your money instantly there are additional fees, free is x4 working days, which is the time it takes to get it to auction I guess? So, hope that's useful to anyone thinking about using them.

20 December 2017

A day's holiday and I'm off to Swindon, catching up with some friends at the MRC before it disappears, and then to Bristol to visit an iPad type Braille lab.

I'm on a brand new GWR train, it smells just like a new car. And would you believe it, it's got problems. We have an engineer on board (we stopped at Royal Oak to pick him-up) trying to restore power to the seats, and heating to the carriages, and fix the onboard kitchen (which is powerless), and fix the announcements which keep doubling up so we are next stopping at "Swindon, Swindon". Sad really. But at least it's running on time so far.

1 January 2018

My first train blog of 2018 is about a tram in Tallinn. It's very clean, it's easy to use, navigation systems are impressive, driver is friendly and speaks better English than I do, there's plenty of Pram and bag space, seats are firm but not uncomfortable and.... there's no excuses over the intercom about the wrong kind of snow, signalling problems or a lack of drivers, it's simply running on time (well ok, 15 seconds late due to a large number getting off at the last stop).

Not only is the driver friendly, so are the people of Tallinn. Genuinely so. The prices are all reasonable and the food is of exceptional quality. There are some impolite people around, but you quickly realise they are visitors from other parts of the former USSR. And it turns out that the British are not disliked, we sent some warships when Estonia was fighting for its independence, and that is remembered fondly by the older generation.

Tallinn has two distinct parts. The old mediaeval town, amazingly well preserved, and the newer city and port. We've spent a good few hours in the old town, discovering fascinating nooks and crannies and insights into history. There are lots of independent coffee shops, and small eateries, as well as some larger chains. Boutique shops and some department stores are in the newer area.

New Year here will give us some ever-lasting memories. Estonians like to sing. And they like to drink. And they like to randomly set off fireworks! HNY!

13 February 2018
Utter confusion on the nearly empty, but new, 08.30 from Paddington to Swindon this morning as there are two A, two B and two C coaches, whilst everyone has been assigned seats in the non-existent coach J.

The train itself is formed of two trains merged together - which means that we have four engines/cabs, maybe back-up if one fails?

The 4 sets of partition doors (presumably necessary to separate the toilet - but actually OTT) are randomly opening and closing. Nobody is near them. The train manager is trying to explain what we should do, which is sit anywhere we like (he's only about ten minutes behind what everyone has already done though) although extra mayhem is being caused by people realising that there is no link between the two trains, and that they are stuck in the rear.

20 February 2018
Caught the earlier train today (no son to slow me down!), and had to stand, but the journey went very quickly because I bumped into another "mature", male, white, grumpy old Human Resources Director who I've known for ages. Apart from the obvious discourse around the state of the world post-Brexit and, hopefully, post-Trump, we talked about the gender pay gap, the inherent inequalities still in existence, more so now for ethnic minorities than for women, and the impact of the Oxfam

Haiti covfefe.

But we settled on an issue that concerns us directly. No, not the issue that we can't get non-exec roles because we are old male and supposedly stale, lol, but the issues surrounding mentorship. The Human Resources world is dominated by women. But many lack confidence and get stuck in mid-level roles, slaves to the rules and procedures and concerned not to take anything but a very calculated risk, for fear of making a mistake and looking foolish.

As male mentors we have both spent many hours over a coffee or a meal helping those women to try things out, push themselves further, challenge the status quo and take steps up the ladder.

Often it's just a simple thing like saying "are you applying for that more senior role" at their current workplace and countering the self-doubt with a reminder that they are more than competent and that, just because the person spec says that experience of trade union negotiations (for example) is desirable ..... it DOESN'T say essential!!!

It's therefore a shame that we both doubt the wisdom of offering to mentor women in the future because, yes, our motives are being questioned. The fall-out from #metoo is that more men are pulling-back from anything but superficial interactions with women in the workplace, especially those in their early career stages, for fear of saying something inappropriate, or being mistaken in intentions.

How can we resolve this, without having to have formal schemes and signed pledges and chaperones at every meeting? Maybe the answer is that we switch to inviting early career stage male, maybe ethnic, mentees instead?

27 February 2018

Today Great Northern excelled themselves. Having heard that here was going to be the 'potential' for bad weather, they implemented a special snow schedule overnight. They then made sure that their website was taken out of service and directed everyone to a holding page which mentioned the tantalising promise of a new schedule, but no clue about the train times. They then looked pretty foolish as the sun shone and the odd flurry of tiny snow-flakes made an appearance. Tweets were hilarious, as people posted granules of salt and explained that the drivers could only safely get in their cabs if the granules melted first.

Later in the day they said that they were attempting to restore a normal service, but what is a normal service? Well it's random cancellations, short trains and anything to blame but themselves (today the signals - Network Rail, at Essex Road, failed so they could stop bothering to serve Moorgate for six hours) and it's drivers not showing up because they are delayed by the snow. WHAT SNOW?

At the moment they are hoping to get the trains back into the right places to provide a full-service tomorrow. Yes. Well. We will see about that. Don't hold your breath.

21 March 2018

Fascinating journey on the bus. So interesting that I stayed on one stop too many, just to make sure I found out what was happening in the seat behind me!

Two men, middle-aged, East London accents, Caucasian, relatively posh accents, were sitting directly behind me.

"So, what you're saying is that it's about a grand a kilo, but for the top grade it's more like twelve hundred?"

Having visited Femke Waltman and Linda Holliday territory recently (The Netherlands), I naturally jumped to the obvious conclusion that this was something you smoked, injected or put in cakes.

Well I was almost right. It did have a cooking theme. When I stood up to go and looked around they were, of course, looking at several different sample bags of Saffron!!!

Instead of helping Trump win his election and Brexit narrowly win the day in Britain, why can't Facebook and Cambridge Analytica do something that would help millions and read my train blogs and sort out the NHS (with a decent pay rise, not this proposed paltry sum that will drive more out), sort out the train companies and help de-stigmatise mental health? Oh, and can they tell me where I left my keys :-(

4 April 2018
"The train is delayed because it is inspecting the tracks". These new 700 class trains are clearly capable of a lot, and don't even need drivers any more. Sadly, they also damage the overhead cables, and so have been banned from using the fast track, which is part of the reason why we have had so many delays recently, in other words it's not just a lack of working rolling stock, drivers and signal and point failures.

My journey back from London today was, however, bang on time and featured a comedian. It was rammed full because it was 4, rather than 8, cars and the previous train had been cancelled. The comedy act was a phone shouter. Apparently, the way that you deal with a poor signal (e.g. going through a tunnel) is to simply shout very, very loudly "can you hear me". Then repeat. Repeat again. Then shout "f**k" and then ask Siri, very loudly, to redial, then shout "f**k" when Siri confirms that there is no signal.

He did get through in the end, and we all learned that it was not his fault that his "b*t*h" had left him, nor that the child had missed school because he was working and she needed to come with him because he was starting early that day, and we learned that everyone was out to get him, even the weather.

Sadly, he had to get off at Hatfield, and those who remained were clearly quite sad to miss the conclusion to the story......

28 April 2018
For those of you who have been wondering why my train blog has failed to materialise in the past month, I've been just had an amazing trip to Ecuador and The Galapagos Islands. I did use the trains to get to, and from, Heathrow and every journey was on time and had the correct number of working carriages, and given that I'd left extra time for a bad experience it meant that I arrived far too early! My travel blog today features great planes and bad boats!

The great plane: there is no direct flight from the UK to Ecuador so you have to travel via the USA (and face the uncertainty of their immigration transit system) or via Madrid on Iberia or, our choice, KLM via Schiphol. What a great choice and what a great airline! Their recruitment and training are top-drawer, their cabins were refurbished and clean, their food was superb, the only marginal thing was the entertainment system .... which was entertaining because it kept resetting. Just meant that I kept everyone around me awake whilst chortling a lot through my umpteenth re-reading of Catch 22 (the HR Directors best friend, second only to The Prince by Machiavelli).

The bad boat: well we chose to visit the Galapagos Islands on a small boat called Galaven. Having never been on a cruise before, I had to learn the etiquette, e.g. it seems like once you have chosen a place to sit at table, you're then stuck with it for 8 days .... unless you are me! I liked the idea that you buy a bottle of wine, and don't have to finish it, but put it aside for the next evening. Galaven was designed to take 18 travellers plus 2 naturalist guides from island to island. Most landings had to use the zodiacs (small inflatable rubber dinghies with an outboard motor) and were either wet landings (you jumped into the sea and walked up the beach, or dry (you jumped onto a rock or cliff face and climbed up), or rarely onto a jetty at the two big populated islands.

Every cabin had a shower (essential given the amount of hot weather walking and snorkelling we were doing) and aircon (essential below decks and near the engine room!). For six of the eight days the boat was OK. Its desalination plant was kaput, so we had to be frugal with water, and the power kept failing for 10 to 20 minutes at a time. But on night six the generator gave up the ghost, and we failed to sleep in hot, humid conditions without light or water (it needed a pump!). So, in the end we went on deck and slept there, and what a great thing it was to do. With no light pollution at all, and no clouds and a new moon, we could look up and see the Milky Way. I didn't get much sleep, but it was truly awe inspiring.

Next day we had to abandon ship, alternative arrangements were made and she went off for a refit. Makes some of the train companies look good in comparison!

18 May 2018
"Morning everyone. All tickets and passes please."
Yes, I'm back on a train again and enjoying people watching. I'm with the non-commuters today. But it's still busy. A whole bunch of people wait for the first off-peak train and pile onto it.

As soon as the "Revenue Protection Officer" emerged from the up-track carriage and made her announcement it was great watching as people suddenly looked guilty and feel for their back pocket wallet or rummage in their bags, sweat breaks out, faces redden, strange excuses utter from their dry mouths. But you can tell they are the innocent ones. Some will have bought two tickets just to be safe!

Yep it's the late teens female in the corner at the other end of the carriage who's going to be the entertainment today. She is being ultra-nonchalant and has just put her feet up on the chair as a final act of arrogance before being found out. But no! I am wrong, it turns out she is one of the inspection team!!!!!!!!

Wow! As an older male tries to walk through to the next carriage she suddenly leaps up with a badge in her hand and asks to see his ticket.

And one other minor amusement. Train boards say "delayed" and automated female announcer says "we are sorry that the 09.41 is delayed", quickly followed by the human in uniform on the platform saying loudly "ignore her - it's not delayed, it's the big white thing with doors in front of you!"

21 May 2018

It would be difficult for me not to comment after two of the worst days on Rail ever, all in the name of a much-improved timetable and service, during which every other train was cancelled and on Sunday and Monday it's down to every 4th train-ish. Not clever. I guess it was silly to ask drivers to volunteer for overtime on the hottest weekend since the last one, when they knew it would be a farce, with trains in the wrong places, revenue protection officers trying to work out what ticket is allowed where etc.

Currently heading to Cambridge on the "new" Thameslink service. I'm sitting on the already infamous ironing board seats. They can pack more people in, and they get their name for being the most uncomfortable seats since the 1890's when third class seats were a simple wooden bench.

But I have a mission! It's to meet up with friends at the Cambridge Beer Festival. So, the return trip will be a lot easier to cope with!!!!!

28 May 2018
GDPR response that I am now sending back: thank you for
sending me a link to your privacy policy and for taking this so
seriously. As a consequence of all this mail I have to deal with, I
am now considered a small business in my own right and I am
about to enter your details onto my database. Please would you
respond and confirm that you are happy for me to hold your
details before you send me any more of your Spam?

And yes, I'm on a train. It's only 8 minutes late so far. It's
rammed full because the prior two were cancelled. The new
timetable hasn't even vaguely settled yet and is causing major
disruption to people's lives. It is so beyond a joke that I have
ceased laughing about it.

8 June 2018
20-minute delay on the intercity Warsaw-Krakow express train
as a consequence of the new tracks being laid over the bank
holiday weekend. Very apologetic train manager, free drinks all
round and our money back if they can't make up the time by
our destination. Ameliorate Thameslink NotGreatNorthern, this
is how it should be done.

27 June 2018
A train blog again, but this time about trains that have
comfortable seats, proper toilets, wood rather than plastic,
friendly station masters and a guard who sells tickets rather
than hands out fines, and the train runs on time of course (they
have trained drivers, and fob-watches that work on this line!).
The Poppy Line. Steam out and Diesel back.

We caught the bus from our campsite in Cromer to Sheringham
Railway Station, and totally surprised the driver by asking for
two returns and brandishing cash. Apparently, he hadn't sold a
ticket for days, it seems that the buses here are largely used by

the over sixties with free bus passes. Quite a community service to run a bus on those terms every half an hour.

Didn't go completely smoothly though. "You can't sit there, that's Betty's seat". And true enough, at the next stop Betty did get on and then she had a good natter.

Tourist steam trains are obviously different from commuter trains. No one is in a rush. Everyone seems to have picnic bags with them. The goods van is rammed-full of push chairs and wheel chairs, no folding bikes to be seen.

Commuter trains feature large numbers of, yep, commuters, all working on laptops or playing on their mobiles, all trying to avoid eye contact. Tourist trains feature lots of adults and children all getting excited and chatting to each other, asking where they are staying and can they recommend a good pub/beach/dog walk/activity.   I know which I prefer. Life is too short......

6 July 2018
I've just been explaining to a couple of tourists that London is always this hot, it's just that we pretend to have cold, wet weather to reduce the numbers visiting us. She promised to keep it a secret, but then said "oh jeez I've posted some sunny photos on Insta, so, so sorry."

5 September 2018
Dear Train-blog Readers, I'm now back from my six months break and I'm starting to look for work to pay the credit card bills, which means that I am reacquainting myself with Ungreat Northern Fail.

I've travelled on trains, planes and automobiles in both Ecuador and many parts of Europe, even Scotland, but all are quite civilised and run to schedules, so it was quite sad to return to a service where people were squashed in, and trains were cancelled, and I quote, "due to the availability of crew". Did they have too many to choose from and just couldn't decide who should drive the stupid thing?

First thing to say is that UK trains seem to be quieter than abroad, as in the people commuting mostly have their heads down in their phones or tablets and don't chat much, whereas the Polish and Italian trains were much more noisy (even in rush hour) as people talked more than they played.

This means that those who make a noise stand out. We had a student, maybe going to college for the first time, who's phone kept going off "yes Mum, we are now at Potters Bar, yes I'm OK" but every 3/4 minutes! The aggravation was the ringtone, I used to like Dancing in the Street!

The funniest was one of my old time favourites, a woman applying lipstick with a compact mirror when the phone went off and yep, she smeared it all over the right cheek :-0

15 September 2018

Whilst waiting for my delayed train yesterday, I had a chat with a cleaner waiting to board. I complimented her work, saying that I had noticed an improvement recently. She explained "well we have half the trains to clean these days and the same number of staff".

Meanwhile back at home I have a serious NEW WORRY. Up until now I have been trying "to kill 99% of all known germs" and been very concerned about the 1% and what they might do to me.

But now Flash have got me concerned about Soap Scum. They tell me that I just have to remove it. Whatever it or they are! But thankfully the product is recommended by Febreze (not quite the same endorsement as my toothpaste - which meets the exacting standards of the royal college of dental surgeons -

but I guess it's a step in the right direction?) so I guess it must seek-out and remove all scum.

If only there was a product that removed racist scum....

28 September 2018
Today I'm riding on the Lesser Spotted Thameslink train, that has somehow managed to get north of Finsbury Park. Sightings like this are very rare, because the senior leaders forgot to train their drivers how to navigate the tracks to Cambridge, something I struggle with, since I always thought that the signalling team actually operated the points?

Back in May, when the true mayhem began, we were told that the service would be interrupted for a short while. Since then it has got worse and they have finally admitted that they haven't employed sufficient drivers (the story that all would be fine after the school holidays ended has been de-mythed, drivers have to be over the age of 18 and so weren't going to school).

I'm now sat on the delayed (of course) train into London. I'm pleased that I have a seat. Even though it resembles an ironing board and may have been designed by Ryanair to encourage people to stand.

In front of me are two older ladies. Neither has remembered their hearing aid, so they are having to shout at each other from close range to be heard. They are discussing Facebook. One is very worried about the photos that her grand-daughter has posted, showing too much flesh apparently. The other says that she doesn't like it on her phone because the videos she "has" to watch are using up her data allowance too quickly.

Even though they are speaking very loudly, neither is listening to the other and the two conversations are running in parallel. It is a joy to listen to.

12 December 2018

There are several reasons that my train blog has taken a holiday. Probably the most important is that the trains had become so unreliable that I switched to driving a car and then linking with the tube, which hurts from an environmental perspective, but buys me many precious hours back in my life.

Second reason is that I've been experimenting with other forms of transport in other countries. Whilst the Tuk-tuk in Cambodia is not the most environmentally friendly alternative to a train, it is certainly way more entertaining, and remarkably quick when you consider its top speed is around 30kph. Quick because Tuk-tuks don't have to obey any laws regarding the road. They switch sides of the road, treat pavements as overtaking lanes and delight in cutting-up other traffic. But you do get there quickly and you don't pay a lot.

The downside of all this non-train travel is that I'm not sitting looking at fellow passengers doing weird stuff. Instead I'm looking out of windows (actually there aren't windows in Tuk-tuks) at people outside doing weird stuff.

And probably the weirdest in Phnom Penh was seeing a motorbike with six passengers on it, another carrying a shed on the back, and then a street food vendor who had set up in the middle of the road and was passing bowls up to drivers as they went past.

On reflection I have a lot of fond memories of Cambodia. The people were very welcoming and genuinely understood the importance of tourist dollars. They called us friends. After the horrors of the Pol Pot regime and the genocide inflicted by the Khmer Rouge (3m out of 8m people died) they have to rebuild, and are doing everything they can to make it a great place to visit. I'd like to go back :-)

16 February 2019
Even the regional trains look the part in central Spain. On time, low ticket cost, full security checks in place, clean and tidy, happy staff and respectful customers. If only.......

4 March 2019
"Breathe the pressure
Come play my game
I'll test ya
Psycho-somatic addict-insane
Breathe the pressure
Come play my game
I'll test ya
Psycho-somatic addict-insane
Come play my game
Inhale, inhale.
You're the victim
Come play my game
Exhale, exhale, exhale"
RIP Keith Flint (we both went to the same school)

29 April 2019
Welcome back to the U.K. says the station announcer, with "we regret to inform you that the train has been cancelled due to a shortage of staff."

After a month of getting used to clean seats travelling in on-time trains in Oslo, New Zealand and Australia, with no mention of Brexit, I am whack back in the middle of it all now!

It's as if I hadn't left. The same issues. The same lame leadership.

At least my fellow passengers are being stoic about the need to change platform for the third time: "needed to get fit"; "who needs the gym"; "they'll do anything to stop us getting bored";

and "at least it isn't raining".

2 May 2019
Back to good old rolling stock. Heater stuck full on. Today it was interesting to watch how fellow travellers handled a testing situation.

Young boy, I'm guessing 4 years old, literally jumps onboard with his mum/carer. He is hyper. Looks like he always is. She looks exhausted. He starts shouting about the best seat to sit on. Mum tries to hush him. Yep. He goes bonkers.

Now given that this kid is already hyper what would you do? Yep, she gives him chocolate! And, I kid you not, full fat Tango to wash it down. Three minutes silence...... then......BOOOOOM SHAKKA LAKKA we are now RUNNING DOWN THE AISLE screaming something like "I'm a train, I'm a train, I'm a train!". One passenger tries the good old distraction ploy. Pulls out an iPad and asks if he has played Angry Birds before? We get 30 seconds silence, then Boom! Runs off again.

Another passenger decides enough is enough, and set- off to find a quieter carriage. This is where the old trains have a distinct advantage over the new single full-length corridor trains.

The mother/carer asks if he wants more chocolate?

At this point an older lady interjects "don't you think he's had enough sugar?" Yep! Mum/carer goes Boom!!!!! "Leave it out! He didn't get any breakfast; he needs his food"

"But that's not food"

"It is, now back-off, before I call my husband!"

Another older lady consoles the first old lady and they also agree to move carriages.

Now just as I wonder what will happen next, it's all over. We pull in to Hatfield and the mum/carer picks up the screaming child "nooooooooooo, noooooo, I want to stayyyyyyy" and off they get.

The two old ladies realise there is no need to leave and return to their seats, to a round of gentle applause! How lovely is that?

7 May 2019
Quite refreshing today to board a train that travelled hundreds of metres down in the Postojna Cave System at a decent speed, with low roof and closed-in walls, without any safety instructions at all, and absolutely no sign of a safety helmet. The complete opposite of some much poorer and smaller caves in the UK where you spend hours dressing up and being given safety talks for absolutely zero danger.

The tour started with a decision for everyone. Which language queue to join. Slovenian an obvious choice for the locals. German for the Germans. French for the French. Japanese for the Japanese. But for the Canadians it was tough. Did they join the British tour, or the American tour? They were quite non plussed!

Once on the train, a story in itself given the desire of all members of Team Japan to want to sit at the very front and nobody was going to get in their way, not even the ice hockey playing Canadians, the fun began. Just as we were starting-off a fellow tourist pushed a selfie stick high up and yes - it got whacked by the tunnel entrance roof!

We stopped and got our first instructions. No selfies on the train and no flash photography. Unfortunately, this instruction was given in Slovenian and English - so only a few people took any notice. And why were we split into language groups, only to be merged back together on the train?

Once deep into the cave, and walking around, the guides had to slowly but surely take out the Japanese and explain about selfie sticks, about keeping up with the tour and about no flash, because it disturbs the Proteus (a salamander like creature that is completely blind, which made me wonder why flash was an issue). No mention of Brexit all day, but lots of congratulations about the new royal baby, for which I genuinely don't think I had any hand in, nor was even aware of, being on holiday.

11 May 2019
I couldn't find the shopping centre at Blyth sea front, even though it was sign-posted! But I have enjoyed my rides on the 308 bus from the camp site to St James Park and back.

As ever, it's the people on the bus that make it interesting. Most fun was a boy aged about 3, with granny and grandad. For some unknown reason they'd bought him a double cone Mr Whippy style ice cream just before getting onto the bus for the 50-minute journey.

He wanted to go upstairs, of course, so granny offered to carry the ice cream. I think the boy was worried that he'd never see it again so he refused. Well that's the polite term for screamed and had a paddy.

We followed them upstairs, avoiding the ice cream smeared steps and hand rail.
Upstairs the sun did it's work and soon the ice cream was literally streaming down the sides of the cone. Boy didn't care. Granny did. Grandad was sensibly in the row behind.

Then we realise she had no wet wipes. No napkins. Just her tiny little ornate handkerchief. Haha! She will learn!

Also. on board were two elderly ladies. They told us that they like the free bus. They travel up and down all day watching the world go by. I bet they have some stories to tell!

16 May 2019

Breaking News! I'm in relatively early for a meeting (a pitch at 8am), and both the train and tubes have been clean and on time and I have had a seat and the people have all been quiet or buried in their phones.

It clearly is possible. Part of my inspiration for writing this is that a long time U.S. based friend called Charlie Sheppard messaged to let me know he was in the U.K. and had just experienced a very reasonable service going up to Cambridge, something he wasn't expecting after reading my train blog for the past few years!

Hopefully some good comes of the blog, and if all goes well there's half a chance of a selfie with the great man if the trains work well and we get to meet up on Saturday! When we last met, we were running around Piccadilly Circus shouting "Hey Dave". It's amazing how many people turn around. I guess in a few years you'll have to shout "Hey Archie" to get the same response. Honestly, I have never seen so much non-sense in the press, and on social media, and on TV about the selection of a name and all the signals the couple were trying to send. Jeez! At least it was a few days relief from Brexit.

Gotta love a good train journey though. Toot toot!

18 May 2019

Today's train update relates to the 14.29 from Staines to Waterloo, stopping absolutely everywhere *en-route*. But if it hadn't stopped everywhere this post would never have had any material or inspiration to work with.

I joined at Staines, and there were about six people in the carriage. They were spread throughout, evenly spaced. Just like at urinals in a large venue. Men naturally spread evenly out and the incoming ones fill the spaces until there's a queue awaiting a place. And that's how it should be.

Now I was sitting by the window in a double seat. Other side of the divide there were 4 free seats, along the next window 3 double seats free and a quadruple.

So WHY THE HECK does weirdo matey boy ask if I can move my coat so he can sit next to me??????!!!!!! For those who need to know he boarded at Twickenham. He didn't seem to be high or inebriated. He didn't smell. But he did fill his entire half of the seat and generated a lot of heat.

What was I to do? Say something? Nope! I'm British and need to be stoic. Change seats? Maybe, but he might follow me. Change carriages? Similar to seats, it would be too obvious.

So mega ploy. Get off at the next station, walk along the platform and get on just before the doors close?! Yes. Small risk of losing a seat, but it's just me today so should be ok.

30 May 2019

Today I was "disappointed" in our train service.

To my American readers this means that I was very, very annoyed. If I were Trump, I would send in the army to sort it out, or build a wall to stop people using it as a means of showing my displeasure to the owners (why aren't the owners the Government?). As Americans you might say "quite" annoyed. (I still remember rewriting a presentation in the States after my NC team said it was quite good - in Britain that means awful - in NC it means very good!) Quite!

It's over a year now and the train operators are having a laugh. They still haven't recruited sufficient drivers. Apparently, they save more by having a reduced wage bill than they get fined for cancelled trains. Not very clever - but then our "Government" has taken its eye off the ball as it makes a mess of Brexit and everything else at the moment. I say "Government" in inverted commas simply because I wish they would (Team USA this is sarcasm, which I think you're learning fast in the Trump era).

Finally, on the train and we travel without any serious hitches (i.e. just ten minutes late, which is something of a decent result) and, sadly, without any weird people to report on. BUT, before you despair, this was more than made up for at the Oval, where I went to see England defeat South Africa in the opening match of the World Cup (unlike the US Baseball "World" Series this features ten different teams from around the world!).

The first weirdness was a man with cricketing Tourette's sitting two along from me. Every time the batsmen played a stroke, even if it was awful, he shouted "shot". On two occasions the batsmen were actually caught out! To the Americans this is similar to someone shouting "Home Run" every single time, regardless of where the ball has gone.

The second was an elderly woman in the queue for a cup of tea (US - a cup of coffee). She arrived after me and then, when I was asked what I wanted by the server, she suddenly said "do you mind, I'm a lady, I should be served first". I have to say that I was quite (very) shocked and so allowed her to order. "I want very, very strong tea, and I want extra milk to prove the tea is strong, and I want to pay the normal price".

By now I was hurting from trying not to laugh, but sadly the assistant failed and sniggered. "You are making fun of me young girl; I want to see the manager".

And so, to the good news. After this exchange I waited back. The assistant was looking sheepish and worried. After the aggressive old lady had said her bit, I explained to her manager what I had witnessed, and said that the assistant was provoked beyond all reasonable doubt, and had behaved beautifully. I got a hug from another lady behind me!

Back to the cricket and, boom, we won!

3 June 2019
Riding on a train
Lulled by locomotion
Falling asleep now
(Haiku for RW)

Travelling on the overground train to Honor Oak. Everyone is well behaved and properly spread out.

A sad reason to travel today. Rob Wallen was a truly lovely guy to work with, and we will all miss him. A sunny day to say goodbye to a man who managed to sprinkle the sunshine and hide his own demons from others. At the wake we all blamed ourselves, but the reality is that you can't stop someone who comes to the end of their tether, unless you lock everyone up in a cell forever.

4 June 2019
Don't leave your will in a safe deposit box at your bank, and certainly not Lloyd's Bank.

This is an update on the story that I told you a couple of years ago after my mum died. Mum had left my sister and I a short note explaining that her will, power of attorney, deeds to her bungalow, and other papers were in a safe deposit box at Lloyd's in Cheltenham.

We went to the branch and were told all boxes had been moved to another branch. Got there to be told the box was missing. And then later that it had been located in a deep storage unit (a salt mine).

Then the killer piece of information. The only person who could access the box was my mum. And in the case of her death we would need a death certificate and a copy of her will to gain access. Mmmmm. But the Will is in the box! Catch 22.

Lloyd's wouldn't budge. So, we lost time and money getting our solicitor involved. Even then all they would do is give her sight of the contents!

So now a few years have passed and probate has finally been sorted (don't ask!). And we have the actual box. AND ON THE BOX IT CLEARLY SAYS THAT EITHER MY MUM OR SISTER CAN ACCESS IT!

Ggggggrrrrrrrrrrrr.   I am now boycotting Lloyd's Bank, again. But the lesson is that you should have a will, it certainly makes it easier for those you love behind to sort things out. And you shouldn't leave the will at your bank!

5 June 2019
Today's train blog features ticket sales and ticket inspectors. Both of whom made my journey much more interesting today.

All the ticket machines, bar one, had failed due to a connection problem (they really must pay their internet provider on time or buy the XL package!), and the bar one had a big queue, as an enlightened elderly gentleman was feeding it 5p and 10p coins out of his trouser pocket. Given the price of tickets I calculated that the ticket window would be the fastest option.

I was right, but only just. I arrived at the window at the same time as the woman in the yellow jacket got to the machine (she joined the queue just after me - is this a British obsession - trying to pick the best queue and then fretting when the other one moves faster?). Actually, it isn't an Italian obsession, they just push straight to the front!

Anyhow, I got my ticket and the older lady behind me took the window as I was putting my things away.

"A return to Welwyn Garden please, with a railcard". "That will be nothing to pay madam, it's free today".

She was so delighted, until she realised, bless her, that she was starting her journey in Welwyn Garden!

And so, to the inspectors. In my carriage they had two people trying to evade payment. I actually want to praise them both. They were so patient. Listening to the lame excuses, taking notes, handling the well-practiced patter, politely pointing out to one of them that this was the third time this month (quite impressive as it is the 5th today) that they had been caught. And then following them off the train at Finsbury Park, where two transport police officers took over.

Oh, the good news. Train was clean and on time.

8 June 2019
An oh too familiar story as I sit at the station and read a note from my boiler insurer. "You need do nothing" should instead say "we hope you won't do anything, so we can get away with this."

Last year we paid £105.60, this year's price has gone up to a whopping £138.00.

I use the old ploy, same as car insurance, same as house contents etc, I phone and say I'm cancelling.

I'm redirected to "a colleague who can help you" who answers the phone as the "retention team" lol. I ask how they can justify the huge percentage increase and (they can't) instead I get "let me look at this". "Actually, we can do this for £92 as you are a valued customer".

Jeez. Enough said. I certainly didn't feel like one. I didn't even have to shop around: please do the same.

9 June 2019

Sad to think that these steam locos at Swanage Railway now have the best punctuality record over the whole network. They also have polite station staff, cleaners who clean and a guard who checks all the doors before blowing his whistle.

26 June 2019

Manspreading. It's not great when a man thinkingly, or unthinkingly, spreads his legs apart to fill both seats on a train (sometimes three seats on the older rolling stock). But the good news is that they are normally wearing trousers and everything is therefore removed from sight, except on the rare occasion when they have an exceedingly large appendage or a colostomy bag - in one case I wasn't sure which, but at least it was still covered.

Womanspreading is though, jeez, so bad that it is worse than buying designer jeans with rips and tears throughout the knees and often higher, it's worse than re-using tea bags or begging with a card reader and smart phone, it's not quite as bad as the lies of a certain leadership contender for number ten, but it is certainly worse than applying makeup, shouting into a phone or sitting next to someone when there are empty seats elsewhere. It is bad because it leaves nothing to the imagination. There is no place to look. All dignity is gone. This "woman" was drinking cider from a can and I was half-expecting to see the processed contents appear lower down.

So, I pretended that I had to get off the train, as I have done a few times before in life, and ended up in my current seat a carriage further down with a view of a chap creating spreadsheets on his laptop, as I head off to meet my super cousin David Tonge, and the delights of Glastonbury.

5 July 2019
Yes! Our trains are delayed "because of high track temperatures at Letchworth". Utterly bizarre since the train we are waiting for is a shuttle between Moorgate and Welwyn!!!!

And, as ever, the driver has come on to the intercom to say the delay is due to signalling problems. So, who knows?

The train itself is clean. It is at the moment. But there are a bunch of lads trying to impress the girls and it could get Lionel. One has such a large hole in his jeans that I thought they were shorts. One of the girls is wearing a high viz jacket. I hadn't realised they were such a fashion item - and on a hot day seems odd - but since when has fashion been sensible or comfortable? And the aircon has just started up. So, we are now getting warmer by the minute. Woohoo!

12 July 2019 Just when I thought everything was going by road, great to see a much more environmentally friendly, lengthy freight train shifting what looks like soil.

And given that it's a hot day to travel I'm pleased to be sitting on one of the old rolling stock trains today with "proper" aircon. In other words, loads of windows that are now open.

The train is very quiet. It's a Friday, so all the work at homers are getting ready for Wimbledon, any real workers got in early to leave at 4pm, and then there's a few of us going in to see Bob Dylan, Neil Young and ZZ Top (I'm in the latter category with

Paul Mez Merrick).   So, everyone is well behaved and chatting about the support acts.   Which if you're going to see Dylan is quite important- since he failed to actually sing the last time I saw him!

4 September 2019
After an uneventful train journey in I've got a gap between meetings and so have popped in to the British Museum. I won't be popping back for a good while, what a dreadful place stuck in the 60's.

A queue for security. Fair enough. Then directed to a till to make a "voluntary" £5 donation. Walk to the courtyard and a large bowl begging for £5. A short walk to the entrance to the Age of Enlightenment and, yep, a security guard stood next to two glass boxes asking for £5. And so, it goes on.

But worse than that, everything is inside a glass case, or it is surrounded by barriers and don't touch signs. Worse than that, many of the old signs that explained what exhibits were have been replaced with an audio guide reference number and just a couple of words.

Nothing interactive, children bored out of their minds and just rows of display cases showing what the Victorians and others pilfered from around the world.

Off to my next meeting (with a £5 cup of coffee) It will save me from this, hopefully.

14 September 2019
Today's commute is on the River Thames ferry, rather than on the train and yes, just like on the train the make-up is being applied, albeit with a far nicer back-drop than an urban train or underground tube.

I've been impressed with the speed that the ferry has gone, but I'm guessing the downside is erosion to the banks. And it's a very pleasant temperature sat outside in the setting sun, unlike the tube which has been hitting the mid-thirties (degrees C) in recent weeks.

No issues with seats, everyone is being very polite, most are tourists with just a few going to the Muse gig at the O2.

5 October 2019
Lunch is sorted as I head to The Albion and then The Pierce Brothers after that with Paul Mez Merrick.   One side of the carriage is stuffed full of people. All with reservations. The other side is empty. Maybe that helps the Pendilino round the corners - a bit like a trapeze on a sailing boat? Stephen Roughley will know if they deliberately fill the eastern side of the train when going north?

Anyhow, I already had to walk half the way to New Street. Coach A was a long way from the gate! But at least they had a defibrillator at the two thirds stage and some staff to encourage the standard seat users on their way.

I'm also quite lucky. I have a lovely lady from Barbados sitting next to me. She is going to see her week-old Grand-daughter for the first time and can't contain herself!

I offered her a Malteser button as she had never tried one before. Nope. She doesn't like it. Hey ho. I do. More for me!

15 October 2019
Today's train journey is badly timed. The schools at Potters Bar have just kicked out and the train is over-run by coughing, sneezing, texting teens.

But it is a bit more interesting than the team who have just visited Tesco HQ in Welwyn. All dressed to the nines. All

91

sporting a wheelie bag filled with presentations, laptop and the essential trendy water bottle with an over large straw attachment.

Their excited chatter after their pitch killed off any thoughts I had that vegetables were supplied by farmers. Nope, this team gave the clear impression that they hadn't ever been outside London (except for trips to Milan and New York and Paris obviously), let alone near a farm! It's all about margins and speed from fork to fork (as if any of their farmers knows what a garden fork is!).

Last week I witnessed another group leaving around lunchtime. Same bags etc. but all much older. I think they had been up to negotiate electronics of some kind. But they were more discrete. One of them looked like he'd been in the trenches, they all took their lead from him. The owner or Chairman maybe?

My reason for writing this? Well blow me over, as I leave the train at Kings Cross there's another lot all waiting to get on, chattering about their pitch tomorrow. I assume they have come a long way and will stay overnight. Sensible. I'm guessing they will be selling shampoos among other things, just because that's what one woman had way too many of in her bag!

And my reason for travelling in? Well I now have a couple of clients in London and so this commute will start being a bit more regular again. Today's about a Mental Health Project, quite appropriate given the week we are in :-)

1 November 2019 Coming back on the train, I tried not to catch the eye of a young half term kid with very sticky fingers who seemed to want to approach every commuter, and instead attempted to read those bits of the newspaper that weren't trying to predict exactly what will happen tomorrow at 9am, or to excuse a poor performance by the Welsh side this morning.

"Britain Deserves Better" came to my attention. Are the Conservative Party being ironic in using this as their main slogan? After nine years of failed promises and bodged projects (the lists are long) are they subtly telling us to vote for some other party at the General election? In 2017 they used "Forward, Together Strong and Stable" which clearly is the exact opposite of what they delivered so can't be re-used.

Labour used "For the many, not the few" last time out and have started with "It's time for real change" in 2019, although I still have no idea on where they stand on the key issues of the day; I don't think you can get elected by trying not to disappoint anyone with anything and remaining on the fence, but we will see.

The Lib Dems ran with "Change Britain's Future" in 2017, but got lost in the fog of internal debate, failed leadership and a generation still smarting from their grants/fees debacle. Having found a new, and quite vocal leader, they want to go with "Stop Brexit" in 2019. I hope they have more to offer than that, as strangely enough I think that a general election should be about more than just Brexit.

9 January 2020
Today I'm attempting to go to Leeds to see an Ideas Foundation collaboration with Burberry and the Northern Ballet, to inspire and give confidence to school and college kids from disadvantaged backgrounds.

I say trying. Hence the train blog is back for a short reprise. At my home station I could only smile when the 06.24 arrived "on time" at 06.27. After the driver had cleaned the windshield, added some water and applied his make-up we set off north, arriving only five minutes late at Stevenage.

Yep. The connecting LNER train was delayed. Then delayed some more. Then cancelled.

Currently I'm on a stopping train to Doncaster, where I apparently will now change and (ticket inspector speaking) "get on the first train to Leeds that is running .... no, I don't know, my system is down and they don't give us timetables anymore". And over the tannoy "we apologise for the delay in this service and the lack of a drinks service today, due to a shortage of staff".

But I know you don't read these train blogs for news of train failures. The interesting stuff is always in the people. And the majority are reading books, papers, playing on phones. I say the majority....

One guy has just decided to go off on one with the ticket inspector/train guard! Sorry I meant "Revenue Protection Officer". "No, I'm not getting off at the next stop". "How are you going to make me?" "Why should I pay for this diabolical service?" "I haven't got to Doncaster on time on my last to 7 trips!"

Yes! I have a travelling companion who will know all about Doncaster.

1 February 2020
Travelling home from a very average football match on the Birmingham to London SS1 Line (slow speed), we've literally just been overtaken by a guy in a wheelchair on the footpath alongside the track.

The carriage isn't full, so there's not a lot to comment on, although I was childishly happy that the Luton fans just missed it by seconds, a whole load of them very well tanked up.

The trip up this morning was livelier. The train was racing past the cars on the M1 and a bunch of late twenties/early thirties women joined us at Coventry. They were on their way to a bender in Birmingham to celebrate the divorce of one of the team (the one wearing her original, and slightly grubby, white wedding dress with an added No Entry sign on the front.

I learned a lot about drinking from them. The idea is to have a small handbag for makeup and cash, and then a rucksack for Prosecco. Each person that is. Then open six bottles at the same time and drink from the bottle. So classy. But so environmentally friendly, no wasted plastic or paper cups for Team Let's Celebrate Divorce Big Time.

I have to say they were rowdy, but very well behaved, and apologetic about a cork bouncing off the ceiling and narrowly missing an older, less than happy, woman who had travelled with me from Euston.

Given that was 11.30 in the morning, I dread to think what state they are in now, maybe re-married? Who knows?

7 February 2020
Sitting on the train into town today, I'm watching a guy doing exercises in the doorway with his two bags. Basically, he's pulling them up to waist height, lowering and repeat whilst singing, out of tune, and clearly unaware that we can hear most of the song through his ear buds, which means he is risking tinnitus I'd have thought. For my female readers I think you'd enjoy watching him. The woman next to me is blatantly staring at him over the top of her Metro newspaper and positively drooling.

And it made me think about the gym I use, which has had an influx of new punters in January, as you would expect.......

I'll start with the one that saddens me most. He comes in and changes, and then goes to the mat. Gets out his towel and water and his own dumbbells. Switching on his iPad he then follows a routine of stretches and push and sit ups, does stuff with his dumbbells in time to the clicks on his iPad. Then 30 mins later packs up and goes. I say sad, because I can't understand why he can't do this at home and save a shedload of cash?

The funniest has to be two lads, one tall and muscular, the other skinnier and less well equipped. They go around the gym together, speaking with Dell-boy type East End accents. The big one says things like "let's kill vis one" and puts the weights to 100kg. Then does the lift 5 times, screams "yes, get in there" and then struts around. The little one then resets to 25kg and does his 5 reps and then high fives the big one. They then move on to the next machine! Entertaining but largely pointless.

My favourite though, is an older lady who is still learning how each contraption works. She is quite frail and I think it's amazing that she is giving it a go. I have learned to look away when she starts asking for help, because I have already heard her life story a couple of times, and it didn't change in the telling. Bless her, she needs help setting the machines at the lowest 5kg setting and then has to work hard to make 6/7 reps. But she doesn't grumble and keeps at it.

The best thing though is that the gym has one constant cleaner, and she is a little bit obsessive about cleanliness. This is a Good Thing! She is amazing. Every day she surreptitiously follows people around cleaning up behind them.

Unlike the trains. Where the crews come and go, there is no pride, and the results are not something to write home about, although it does mean there's a free paper for me to read on the seat opposite me, once I can take my eyes off superman.

8 February 2020

Sitting on the first off peak train is much more fun, when you choose to play the mental game of "why is this person travelling on the train today?

There are some that are obvious, so let's rule out the two ladies who have already given the game away by discussing which shops they will go to first, and whether they will take the Victoria or Piccadilly line. We can also rule out the school uniform child, although we could play a secondary game of "why are they so late?"

You could also rule out the guy in workman's clothes with a tool box. But, actually, this is quite interesting. From the state of his overalls he's not a plasterer, nor a decorator, and there's no grease or oil staining. I'm thinking electrician, because the size of his toolbox isn't large enough for carpentry tools.

Across the way is a plonker. I've seen this guy before. He brings a folding bike on board with him and insists on making the entire journey in his helmet and full Eddie Merckx (yes young ones you'll have to look up who this is) retro cycling gear. He has an overly large rucksack. He has some kind of office job, because I have seen a pair of black shoes in the side pockets, and his hands show no signs or manual work, but there is no way he is customer facing. Geeky, so maybe high-end IT?

More intriguing today is a young woman who is really smartly dressed, hair and makeup immaculate, sitting opposite-me and looking nervously at a folder with about 20 pages of paper in it. I am so tempted to ask if she wants to practice some interview questions before she goes in! I chicken-out, but when she stands-up at Finsbury Park, I simply say "good luck", and she turns her head and says "thanks". Awwwww.

11 February 2020
Given that this train is as empty as any train I've ever been on, it's difficult to give a commentary on human behaviour.

Instead I will have to settle for part two of the gym observations.
Today I had a business call at 8am, so entered the gym after 9am. Quite a different crowd.

There was a steady trickle of women coming in. Some singly, and others in pairs. I'm guessing they had just dropped the kids off at school and were popping in before their next chore. Very few (as in zero) men.

One was clearly there to be serious about her fitness. She jogged in and jumped up onto the running machine, and set off at a pace that would leave me behind. What made the viewing interesting (from my bike), was that she slowly stripped off as she heated up. But fair play, she was a serious user for a good 50 minutes (and was still going when I left).

Next to her was an older woman who had set a high incline at walking speed. She was hanging on to the machine for dear life, negating the whole point of the incline. After a few minutes she let go and, quite gracefully, slid back to ground level and then spent the time it took me to do 3 sets of reps on two machines, filling and drinking from her water bottle, before towelling-off and disappearing. She was there for a good 15 minutes in total. But I guess that is more than most.

Two bikes away from me is a mid-twenties woman going through a routine. Slow, fast, slow, fast. It involves a lot of peddling, obviously, but also a lot of fiddling with her phone. Thank goodness she isn't actually going anywhere; she would be mowing them down by now.

As I approach the abs machine at my stately, elderly pace I am overtaken by two women who claim it 4 meters before I arrive. The reason this is annoying, is that I do have my little routine, and whilst it can cope with one person getting in the way for a few minutes, it struggles when two people decide to discuss the state of the swimming pool, whilst doing nothing on the blessed machine, except for one of them sitting on it! Grrrr.

I think I'll just try to get there earlier next time.

13 February 2020

I didn't commute yesterday, so you get the combined musings of two days of observing the early morning gym users as I sit on my slow-moving train into London today.

Tattoo man Is an early bird. He wears an unnecessarily small wife-beater vest, which allows us all to see both the rippling muscles and the Chinese dragons on his shoulder blades. He works exclusively in the weights area, mostly with his arms, and occasionally legs (I hope not to meet him on a dark night or, if I do, that he will remember me!). When not pulling up several hundred kilos at a time he's drinking protein shakes, or towelling himself down, a bit like those self-flagellating pious religious types of days gone by, and movies featuring that guy who played the lead in Big.

Now let's move onto cycling man. He is equally amazing. He is currently on a time trial in the French Alps and is wearing the leaders yellow top. He is literally standing up and pumping his legs like nobody's business. His face is puce red. He is breathing very heavily. A sneaky look, and he's on the top setting which I can barely make move. I check where the defibrillator is, just in case.

Over in the far corner there is commotion. I can't claim to have seen it happen sadly, but a couple of younger lads (who work at Sainsbury's) were shadow boxing. It's a good work out and very healthy, normally. But one has actually decked the other. I pretend to cough to cover up my laughter, but then everyone stares at me trying to work out if I have Covid-19 I guess.

I'm saved by the muzak pumping out a louder version of "everyone likes to party" in the background. And I'm thinking "actually they don't, I know many introverts......"

Now back on the train I'm google searching why I am gaining weight. Surely, I should be losing weight after about 4 months of dedicated gym-ing? Apparently not. The answer is that muscles are heavier than fat, lol. Denies the cakes and coffee that I reward myself with, me thinks!!!!!

19 February 2020
My train blog today is going to be about etiquette. Why? Well let me start many years ago.... when I was at Primary School I was presented with a "Courtesy" Badge, because I ran (ironically, against all the rules) to open the door for a teacher. And that's how I thought you were meant to behave. My Aunt scolded me for not cleaning my nails, and .... but that's for another blog.

Today the world is a very different place. I stood aside as the train door opened to allow a woman to board. The first reaction, a shove in the back from the guy behind me, was to be expected and was quite normal. As the train arrived, he had been anxiously counting the empty seats through the windows and was getting agitated. When the train stopped five yards short of where he assumed the door would be, he mildly lost the plot. And when I didn't board immediately, he felt a shove was in order!

The second reaction I didn't expect, and it led to a minor confrontation, and the guy behind me gasping. The woman I had stood aside for said "don't patronise me, get on for heaven's sake!". The confrontation wasn't with me (I'm meek and mild as you all know). It was with another woman behind the woman who I was letting on, who said "ridiculous, get on!". So, we all went for it at the same moment and squeezed in, and then spent the next few minutes trying to sit as far apart as possible and not look at each other. Hence why I am now writing my blog in a cathartic kind of way, staring down at my screen.

Train etiquette tips:
•Please don't rush for the doors and cram in, there is always time. I think I was told that courtesy costs nothing (not strictly true in a queue with limited supplies).
•Once you board, take seats as far from others as reasonable, spreading out, but not manspreading, obviously.
•If the train is already very busy, then it is fine to throw a coat or a bag from one end of the carriage to the other to bagsie your seat.
•If this fails, then stand as close as you can to the person who took the last seat, and make them feel as uncomfortable as you can (a good tip is to read a paper and bash it in their face).
•If things get tight then start to turn around fast, your rucksack will now randomly hit people and create space for you.
•Failing that, pretend to make a loud phone call and ensure that the signal keeps failing so that you say the same inane thing again and gain …. and again.
•Although not always possible at short notice it is great to open up a McDonalds at this point, and accidentally squirt the red sauce everywhere.
•If you forgot to bring fast food with you, then chewing gum loudly, with your mouth open, is a substitute, but it's hard to recreate the smell of fast food, unless you ate something quite unpleasant the night before of course.
•As a female you can start doing your hair and make-up, whilst a male scratching your crotch is quite effective.
•If you have a drink, then slurp or sip it loudly, and as soon as it is nearly finished don't bother looking for bins (they will be full anyway), instead place it carefully next to the foot of the target,

and then a little while later knock it over, accidentally of course, when the train sways or stops.

27 February 2020
Today I'm sat in a rammed commuter train to London, but at least I have a seat. Cheerily we have already been told to expect delays because one of the new trains ahead of us has broken down (again).

Opposite me are two women who are excitedly discussing the first snow of the year. They have progressed from how wet the snow has made their fashionable, but completely unsuitable, coats, to their concern for the blackbird chicks and whether or not they will survive.
One of the pair is so animated that her arms are whirring like windmills. Unfortunately, however, it's not her hands I have noticed, it is an early expectation of dribble from the corner of her mouth trickling down and adding to the state of dampness of the coat (navy colour and a wool mix, it will smell of damp sheep soon!).

I hate when I see something like that. I now have to spend all my time trying not to look at it! Having seen James McEvoy in the excellent National Theatre production of Cyrano de Bergerac at the cinema recently, I remember how difficult it must have been for those speaking to him not to either look at, or mention his nose.

As their conversation moves on to the different types of snow, I kick myself for not having charged my noise cancelling headphones over-night, whilst thinking about the more serious issue of whether or not this will constitute a reason for Useless Northern Abellio to cancel trains home later tonight? It might well be the wrong kind of wet snow, after all.

10 March 2020

Today's train journey is akin to the photos of Milan in lockdown. A usually busy train is empty. I guess everyone is queuing for toilet rolls and therefore can't actually get in to work today?

Before I got the train, I went to the gym and it made me think about germs and general virus spreading techniques. Luckily our gym has sanitiser wipes and a superb cleaner who works tirelessly to keep it clean. But some people try their best to undo the good work. I thought I would reprise my train etiquette blog of a few weeks ago as a gym blog today, here goes....

On entering the gym sneeze all over the door handle, this will have a decent effect, and then wipe your hands on the water fountain for good measure. Save the environment: rather than wasting tissues, use a manky hanky to wipe down equipment that you have used, make sure it's damp by blowing your nose into it first.

And then some non-Covid gym tips:
 * Always look confident on a machine, even if you have never used it before.
* Use your dirty towel to hide the fact that you are reducing the weights from 75kg down to 15kg when you get on, and then again putting it back up to 100kg before you move to the next machine. * Always wear appropriate clothing, "wife beater tops" for men are outstanding, for example, as are jeans with a bikini top for women (yes, I kid you not, I regretted not having my phone camera with me).
* Breaking wind on some machines does happen, just let out a hearty "yeah" at the same time and punch the air, that should cover it up.
* If you are waiting for a machine, stand half a meter away and start coughing, without covering your mouth, the machine will soon be free. Alternatively, just stand close and keep looking at your watch and then them.

* Always sit on a popular machine to send emails, take phone calls and play mobile games, it helps others learn how to control their temper.

* Leave items of clothing or water bottles on each machine that you visit, hence keeping others away, and again helping them control their blood pressure.

12 March 2020
As I sit on the train today to attend the legendary Prof Tumani Corah's celebration of his KBE, I am surrounded by super carriers (yep the schools have kicked out half an hour ago and the kids are coughing all over the place!), whilst I read lots of emails from suppliers.

Such as "we are now cleaning our reception area twice a day"; "we are cleaning our toilets more frequently, especially the taps"; and "if a member of our hotel staff is unwell we are quarantining them, rest assured it is safe to stay with us".....
.......it makes me wonder whether these places were ever safe to visit before!

14 March 2020
I was looking forward to WBA v Birmingham. A decent bit of rivalry and a song-song.

On Thursday the Government said go ahead with mass gatherings for at least another week, presumably because they wanted more people to catch the disease before putting the dampers on?

So, I got my train tickets, trying to be environmentally friendly, but also meant I could have a beer after the game with fellow baggie Paul Mez Merrick.

Then the football authorities took matters into their own hands (sanitised no doubt) and stopped the leagues. At the same time the Government decided to stop testing most people (ministers and football players excepted), and asked us to stay at home, wash our hands, and look at their web site.

I guess stopping testing means that we will see a slowing in the curve and the sombrero will become a top hat (that will please Jacob Rees Mogg). But more importantly for my train blog readers, you are now denied 4 train journeys, 2 tube journeys and 4 Metro Tram journeys. Sorry about that. We will all have to imagine what people would have done in those various carriages to entertain us!

18 March 2020

I guess this is my first Train Blog without Trains. No trips needed because everyone is working from home or being laid-off.

Two of my smaller clients that I was working with have just been told by their investors that they have to wind-up this week, so I'm going to be helping with quite a few more cv's, albeit the chances of getting a job at the moment will be tiny.

Rather than a train ride, I took a walk into town. Roads were quiet, and I could cross without waiting for the lights, spaces for cars everywhere, where normally there would be none.

Once in town I was pleasantly surprised by the number of shops, restaurants and cafes still open, even if they were mostly empty (how long can that last?). I do think it disingenuous of the PM to say that he recommends we don't go to these places, rather than closing them, and thus invalidating their insurance.

I was fascinated by the queues that were forming. A great example being at the bank, where the queue would normally be scrunched up inside the building, it had now spread out to the pavement, with everybody keeping a meter or two away from the next person in line.

And it was interesting to note just how many people were wearing gloves on a mild day, apparently, they have been selling like hot cakes. The difference between them and toilet rolls, is that they actually might serve a purpose.

Annoyingly, there was an older woman coughing in the paper shop, the daggers thrown her way were extreme! She suddenly went red as she remembered to put her hand in front of her mouth (yes, I know it's meant to be her elbow, but this was a start). She then muttered something and walked out. I'm not sure if she had paid for her Daily Mail (says a lot!), but it was obvious that the guy behind the till didn't want to call her back, or talk to her again, a wise decision.

On the way home I saw several groups of friends, couples, talking to each other in hushed and earnest tones. In one case they were taking up the entire footpath by trying to keep their distances from each other. On a positive note, the daffodils and tulips are all out, there is blossom in some trees, lots of buds everywhere, and the family tortoise, Ron, has arisen from his hibernation and clearly living a good life, oblivious of the crisis amongst the rest of us.

22 March 2020
On a good long walk in the non-train-blog-blog, sunshine today and sad to see that a huge oak has fallen foul of the very gusty wind last night. Impressive to see a team from HERTS CC out so quickly to deal with it. We've had floods since the New Year, high winds and now pestilence. Maybe the environment is wreaking its revenge.

Walking around is a strange experience, as most people go to exaggerated lengths to steer clear of me, crossing to the other side of the path, or in one case leaping into a bush as if I were an articulated lorry.

My response has been to say "hello", or "good morning" quite loudly.

Of approximately 100 people I have walked past, I would say that about a third look scared, put their heads down and start walking more quickly, clearly worried that if they respond I might want to have a chat with them! Another third, but mostly the older ones it seemed, responded and kept walking. And the final third gave no reaction whatsoever, as if they were in their own world and had never heard me.

Hopefully all this is just temporary and we can get back to chatting and being social again, sooner rather than later.

25 March 2020

I am really looking forward to my first train ride, post Covid. And that's yet another thing that I never thought that I would say before all this started. In the same way that a simple bunch of daffodils makes the room I'm now living in so much more bearable.

It is increasingly difficult for me to comment on directly observed human behaviour right now. Yesterday's walk was uneventful, occasionally passing dog walkers or parents exercising their children, the odd couple, but all at a safe distance, and 100% either replied back or nodded when I said 'Hi' or 'Good Afternoon' to them.

The sun and a hint of warmth has brought out the ants in our back garden. So, I started watching them instead of Homo Trainicus. They are the total extreme opposite of social distancing. They had formed a long line going back and forth from their nest to a scrap of food. As each passed one another they touched antenna and moved on. Some were carrying, some must have been using their social stomachs. I was thinking that if you introduced a virus into one, they would all have it within minutes.

I was then rudely snapped-out of my mesmerising ant encounter by a scuffle between two squirrels. Interestingly (well to me anyway!) they didn't actually scratch each other, but they did raise themselves up and shouted a lot. Then one (my squirrel, it's in my garden!) suddenly started to move fast along the top of the fence towards the other.... and instead of a fight the other squirrel turned and legged-it. Tyson Furry, as he shall now be known, stopped, sitting on top of the fence, looking rather pleased with himself and started preening. About a minute later he was joined by his partner and then they ran around the fence, up the tree, down the tree, up the fence and then back on the ground, running in circles, oblivious that I was watching. Another three minutes of this and Tyson confirmed that he was the male!

The only other event of note in all this is that our friendly robin (who always comes to say 'hello' to me when I am digging, or planting, or mowing), came and stood near me. I pointed to the ants, but he wasn't interested. A bit like a Labrador begging for a walk I couldn't stand it any longer and so went and turned over a bit of soil, and instantly created a very happy robin.

27 March 2020
If you have a doctor, nurse, care worker or other essential worker living nearby, please offer to take their dog for a walk or simply drop round an occasional care parcel containing milk, bread and some goodies.

Because many of their colleagues are either sick or having to self-isolate, they are having to work extended shifts, and quite often they are either too knackered to go shopping, or the shops are shut when they finish.

Please share this (I've never said that before), or send similar words out with your own favourite dog picture and tag me so that I can like it.

For my blog fans, no trains were hurt in the making of this post.

29 March 2020
Almost two weeks without a train journey to report on, and yet lots of other things are happening, and I'm most certainly learning. Here's some random points:

• Hand cream is more important than toilet rolls
• You can be an executor to the wills of several elderly relatives all in one week, as the constant news about age-related deaths makes them anxious
• People do respond to massive change when given the facts and have things explained
• Some people never, ever listen, or are incapable of listening, and my good nature can be taken advantage of as a consequence • Firms that used to pay their bills in 30 days are now using this as an excuse to take 60 days and counting
• Hotels dot com are useless in a crisis, whilst Airbnb score an OK • Margaret Thatcher was a milk snatcher, but Jeremy Hunt was far worse, he oversaw and encouraged the destruction of the NHS just before we needed it
• Celebrities and footballers and politicians can get tested in seconds for covid, health workers in weeks
• Americans got what they voted for, so did we (exiting Europe just when we needed it)
• Countries use this event to hide stuff that we would normally be up in arms about (c.f. Palestine)
• I did have a book in me, and now three have all come out at once, just a shame that publishers are now overwhelmed
• I still don't like gardening
• Doctors and Nurses are putting themselves at real risk every day because our Government let them down, they still don't have the right PPE in the right places

- Stormtroopers armour is about as effective as a surgical mask
- I really miss live Gigs and Sport; live streams and replays of old games don't do it for me
- Netflix has procured some real dross, finding the pearls is tough going
- I really fancy a pint of real ale (out of a bottle or a tin is not good enough)
- Long hair is going to be a trend
- A lot of people have pictures of beaches on their phone
- Too many people like or share stuff without reading it first, lol

If all this goes on too long, I will get my childhood train set out and take you through the experience. You have been warned!

2 April 2020

My regulation daily walk yesterday was, of course, not to the railway station, but instead to the woods near where I live. Yep, I know, I'm very lucky, and I do feel for those of you self-isolating in a flat in a city, where the parks have been closed.

The first thing that I noticed, largely because it screamed at me from a great height, was a Red Kite. I've never seen one in this area before, so I stood gawping at it, watching it glide, then flap and soar higher, to relax and glide again. It was magical!

If fact it was so magical that I probably contravened all the rules by just standing still and not exercising (I can never spell that word, ggrrr). When it decided to move on to another territory, I took the hint and moved on. Sorry I can't tell you how it swooped and picked up a vole, that would be lying!

I passed several couples, with whom I exchanged a 'Hi' or 'hello' or 'Good Afternoon', several cyclists (not even a grunt, just head down mindless record breaking runs through the paths using their special knobbly tires), and a lot (as in more than ten), of dog walkers who were either shouting so much at their dog to behave that they didn't notice me, or in one case shouted at me not to touch their dog in case I contaminated it!

I wasn't sure what I was going to contaminate it with, but that has got me thinking if ever I meet them again!!!!

Anyhow, the real interest was about two thirds through my walk in an area where bikes couldn't go and dog walkers hadn't chosen to go, and that couples would have to walk in single file through, and so didn't bother.

A lone, middle-aged woman, earnestly talking on the phone, endlessly sweeping her longish hair back with her free hand. I don't think that she heard me approaching, because it was clear that she was trying to have a chat with her current affair, obviously some way away. She was talking about how awful it was living with "him", "cooped-up with his mother" and not being able to get away and that she was "desperate to have you in my arms again soon".

At which point I said "Hiya!" as I walked past. Talk about a red face!!!!!! Lol, lol, lol.

I guess that the family lawyers might well be busy when we are allowed out again!

9 April 2020
My old slippers died. Apparently, they aren't built for continuous use during lockdown nor, indeed, gardening.

I tried to buy some replacement Skechers, but everyone else obviously had the same problem, because they were sold out everywhere, and I can't fit into a size 5, and a size 12 falls off.

I therefore looked for the cheapest pair online, just to see me through.

They were awful! They were too tight and kept rubbing the top of my foot. That's what happens when you buy cheap products,

I thought.

But no! This morning I couldn't get my foot into one of them at all, and it turns out both had cardboard packaging inserts in them, to help them keep their shape in transit!

Now removed, they are quite comfortable and so, off to do some digging.

11 April 2020
Krakatoa erupts - and the BBC and Skye News apps have nothing to show except covid-19. What other news stories are going un-reported?

I'm not going to be travelling by train "for the foreseeable future" in "these unprecedented times", to quote two of the most popular phrases being spouted by politicians at the moment.

This is the point that I need to put the train blog on hold whilst I write it up and get it published.

I'm going to donate all profits from this book to the NHS Charities Together appeal. Not to prop up a poorly funded NHS, but to go to the charities that make life a bit easier for the staff and patients.

Fitting on a day when the UK Government has finally admitted that it hasn't managed to get the right PPE in all the right places at the right time, let alone ordered enough testing kits and reagents to meet it's promise.

Stay at Home. Stay Safe. Protect the vulnerable and the essential workers. Save the NHS.

Printed in Germany
by Amazon Distribution
GmbH, Leipzig